Breath of Spring

A Comedy in Three Acts

Peter Coke

A Samuel French Acting Edition

SAMUELFRENCH-LONDON.CO.UK
SAMUELFRENCH.COM

Copyright © 1959 by Peter Coke
All Rights Reserved

BREATH OF SPRING is fully protected under the copyright laws of the British Commonwealth, including Canada, the United States of America, and all other countries of the Copyright Union. All rights, including professional and amateur stage productions, recitation, lecturing, public reading, motion picture, radio broadcasting, television and the rights of translation into foreign languages are strictly reserved.

ISBN 978-0-573-01053-8

www.samuelfrench-london.co.uk

www.samuelfrench.com

FOR AMATEUR PRODUCTION ENQUIRIES

UNITED KINGDOM AND WORLD
EXCLUDING NORTH AMERICA
plays@SamuelFrench-London.co.uk
020 7255 4302/01

Each title is subject to availability from Samuel French,
depending upon country of performance.

CAUTION: Professional and amateur producers are hereby warned that *BREATH OF SPRING* is subject to a licensing fee. Publication of this play does not imply availability for performance. Both amateurs and professionals considering a production are strongly advised to apply to the appropriate agent before starting rehearsals, advertising, or booking a theatre. A licensing fee must be paid whether the title is presented for charity or gain and whether or not admission is charged.

The professional rights in this play are controlled by Film Rights Ltd in association with Laurence Fitch Ltd, Suite 306 Belsize Business Centre, 258 Belsize Road, London, NW6 4BT.

No one shall make any changes in this title for the purpose of production. No part of this book may be reproduced, stored in a retrieval system, or transmitted in any form, by any means, now known or yet to be invented, including mechanical, electronic, photocopying, recording, videotaping, or otherwise, without the prior written permission of the publisher. No one shall upload this title, or part of this title, to any social media websites.

The right of Peter Coke to be identified as author of this work has been asserted by him in accordance with Section 77 of the Copyright, Designs and Patents Act 1988

BREATH OF SPRING

Produced at the Cambridge Theatre, London, on 26th March, 1958 with the following list of characters:

(*in the order of their appearance*)

MISS NANETTE PARRY ("NAN")	Hazel Hughes
BRIGADIER ALBERT RAYNE, C.B., C.M.G., M.V.O.	Michael Shepley
LILY THOMPSON (the maid)	Joan Syms
ALICE, LADY MILLER	Mary Merrall
DAME BEATRICE APPLEBY, D.B.E. ("BEE")	Athene Seyler
MISS ELIZABETH HATFIELD ("HATTIE")	Elspeth Duxbury
PAPE	Antony Baird
KEMP	David Chivers

SYNOPSIS OF SCENES

The action of the Play passes in the living-room of Dame Beatrice's flat overlooking the Albert Memorial

ACT I
An evening in Spring

ACT II
Six months later. Early afternoon

ACT III
Six months later. Afternoon

Time—the present

ACT I

SCENE—*The living-room of Dame Beatrice's flat overlooking the Albert Memorial. An evening in spring.*

It is an old-fashioned, second-floor, mansion flat with french windows across the corner up L, *leading to a balcony overlooking the Albert Memorial. Double doors up* C *lead to the entrance hall, across which the front door can be seen, with a corridor beyond giving access to the lift, other flats and staircase. There is a fireplace, with a "cosy-stove" down* R. *A door down* L *leads to Beatrice's bedroom. Originally the drawing-room, it now also houses some of the dining-room furniture. The result is an overcrowded, cheerful, slightly antiquated room, crammed with furniture and mementoes from China and India. There is a desk with a telephone and elbow chairs down* L; *a tub chair* LC; *an oval table up* LC; *and a plant-table in the window. A cupboard for drinks stands* L *of the double doors. There are upright chairs* R *and* L *of the doors,* L *of the drinks cabinet and at the downstage end of the oval table up* LC. *A plinth at the downstage side of the curtains has a secret cupboard in it. A beer crate stands at the downstage end of the plant-table. There is a sideboard up* RC, *with a folded screen down* R *of it. In front of it is another table with plants. An ottoman stands* RC *with a small table behind it and a rug with an animal's head on the floor in front of it. There is a small table above the fireplace and a cabinet below it. A fireside stool stands in front of the stove. Down* R *is an armchair with a paper rack below it. At night the room is lit by table-lamps on the desk down* L *and on the table above the fireplace. A small table, with a bowl of ferns stands in the hall.*

When the CURTAIN *rises, it is about half past seven on an April evening. The lamps are lit and the stove is burning, but the window curtains are not yet closed. The double doors up* C *are open.* MISS NANETTE PARRY *is standing by the desk, speaking on the telephone. She is a gaunt, enthusiastic lady who dresses peculiarly and has a deep booming voice.*

NAN (*into the telephone*) Yes; yes . . . But, Henrietta, this is the second time in three weeks that you've cancelled your voice lesson. (*Severely*) You're never going to get rid of your strange vowels that way. (*Sympathetically*) Oh, you poor beast. I understand. (*She sits at the desk and consults her note-book*) Well, can you manage next Monday at the same time? . . . (*Annoyed*) Well, get your book and look. (*She waits*)

(BRIGADIER ALBERT RAYNE, C.B., C.M.G., M.V.O., *enters the hall by the front door. He is a distinguished-looking, white-haired and moustached, elderly gentleman, still with a military bearing, who though frequently short-tempered and dictatorial, has beautiful manners, and is charmingly courteous in an old-fashioned way. He is carrying a foolscap board on which some papers are clipped. He takes off his hat and comes to the double doors*)

BRIGADIER. Oh. (*He is displeased at finding Nan*) Good evening, Miss Parry.
NAN (*displeased at the interruption*) Oh, it's you, Brigadier.
BRIGADIER (*moving* C) Is Beatrice back?
NAN. Not yet.
BRIGADIER (*peeved*) Nuisance; wanted to show her my findings. (*He puts his hat, gloves and umbrella on the left end of the ottoman. Enthusiastically*) I've had a splendid day.
NAN (*not interested*) Oh?
BRIGADIER. I've travelled backwards and forwards between Hyde Park Corner and Hammersmith *eight* times.
NAN. I thought you did that yesterday.
BRIGADIER. I did! But that was on the *seventy-three* bus. Today I was on the *nines*. There's all the difference. As I am very soon going to point out to London Transport headquarters.
NAN. Really.
BRIGADIER (*moving to* R of *Nan*) My plan will completely eliminate this absurd bunching and long gaps. (*He enthusiastically shows her his board*) This is my table of minute by minute timings along the route. Blue for the seventy-threes: red for the nines.
NAN (*into the telephone*) Yes. But hold on a minute.
BRIGADIER. The differentiation of timing is staggering . . .
NAN (*crossly*) Well, I can't be staggered now; I have a pupil on the line.
BRIGADIER (*staggered*) But surely my plan is more important than . . . ?
NAN (*interrupting*) Do you mind?
BRIGADIER (*collecting his hat, gloves and umbrella; very offended*) Well, please report immediately Beatrice returns. (*He moves to the double doors*) She'll be interested in my findings. (*In his best military voice*) All right, carry on.

(*The* BRIGADIER *exits by the double doors to* R)

NAN (*into the telephone*) Now, Henrietta . . . Good. And mind you put in some practice before then. Have you been doing your exercises? . . . Let me hear some reduplicated consonants . . . (*She leans back to listen*) Yes, yes. Come along. The "P's" . . . No, no, no. (*She demonstrates*) Hop Poles. Soup Plates. Plump Partridges. Repeat . . . Fair. Now the "D's". Bad Dog. Bigoted

Dotards. Muzzled . . . (*She breaks off suddenly*) I'm giving you a free lesson: I'm mad.

(*The front-door bell rings*)

(*She rises guiltily and lowers her voice*) I must go. Monday, then, at three-fifteen. Knowing Byron's *Lamentation Over Greece*. (*She replaces the receiver and creeps up* L *to* L *of the double doors, then darts to* R *of the doors*)

(LILY THOMPSON *enters the hall from* R. *She is a cheery, down-to-earth, very attractive girl with a slight Cockney accent. Her brusque manner does not conceal her great love for Bee, and to a lesser degree for the others, whom she treats as children*)

LILY (*catching sight of Nan*) Hi! What are you doing in there?
NAN (*evasively*) A telephone call.
LILY (*moving into the room*) You lodgers really are a menace.
NAN. Lily! (*She moves to* R *of Lily*) Dame Beatrice told you not to refer to us as lodgers. We're guests.
LILY. Guests, squatters, lodgers; I don't mind.

(*The bell rings again*)

Oh, don't be so impatient. But what I do mind—is you all flocking in here turning Dame's private quarters into a telephone booth.
NAN (*picking up a textbook from the table behind the ottoman*) Dame Beatrice said we could use the telephone.
LILY. Occasionally. In the mornings. Not buzzing in and out like a whole lot of damn bees in a hive.
NAN (*ominously*) Lily, if I'd spent three years in—(*emphasizing*) you-know-where—I'd be more careful of what I said to people.
LILY. If you'd been three years in clink you'd be even further up the "hop pole".

(NAN *stamps out by the double doors to* R. *As she does so the bell rings again*)

All right, I'm coming as fast as I can. (*She goes leisurely to the front door and opens it*)

(ALICE, LADY MILLER, *enters excitedly by the front door. She is still pretty with the aid of coiffeur and beautician, and elegantly though not expensively dressed. When the front door is open there is the noise of the party from the flat next door*)

ALICE (*as she enters*) Sanctuary, Lily, sanctuary!
LILY (*surprised at seeing her*) Oh, hullo, my lady. (*She closes the front door*)
ALICE (*coming into the room*) Whoever are those ghastly people out there? I had to fight my way out of the lift.
LILY (*moving to* L *of Alice*) They're from the next-door flat, my

lady. (*She takes Alice's hat and coat*) Mr Spanager's giving one of his cocktail do's.

ALICE (*moving below the ottoman*) He must serve stronger drinks than my friends ever do.

LILY. He's a rich stockbroker. (*She puts Alice's hat and coat in the hall*) He's always giving parties. Calls it "ploughing back the profits". (*Eagerly*) How was Le Touquet, my lady? Did you have a gorgeous gamble?

ALICE (*with a gesture of horror; in a whisper*) Shh! Don't mention it, Lily. Where's Dame Beatrice? Don't tell me she's next door sipping profits? (*She sits on the ottoman*)

LILY (*moving to* L *of the ottoman*) No, my lady. She's out at one of her charity committees.

ALICE (*with mock alarm*) Poor darlings, I bet she's giving them hell! How is she?

LILY. Well, she hasn't been up to anything lately. (*She moves to the windows and closes the curtains*) It's worrying. I get fussed when she's quiet. It means something's going to blow up.

ALICE. Don't I know! The first time I met her she was quiet.

(LILY *crosses to the sideboard, collects a tablecloth, cutlery and table-mats and returns to the table up* LC)

Ten minutes later she had me parading between sandwich-boards in front of Buckingham Palace.

LILY (*laughing*) Don't tell me you was a suffragette? (*She commences to lay the table*)

ALICE. All Dame Beatrice's friends had to be suffragettes.

LILY (*convulsed with laughter*) I can just see you all marching along.

ALICE. Don't you laugh too soon. (*Ominously*) Has she given up the idea of adopting children?

LILY (*immediately sobered*) No. We still hear a lot about them.

ALICE. How many now?

LILY. Five. Assorted colours.

ALICE. We must trust to luck they'll blow over. (*She powders her nose*) While I'm waiting, I might as well see the Brigadier. Is he in?

LILY (*warningly*) I wouldn't if I was you. We've got a third lodger since you've been away . . .

ALICE. A third?

LILY. A Miss Hatfield. She mends china. At least, that's what she calls it; the cup she did for me fell straight to pieces again.

ALICE. What has that to do with my not seeing the Brigadier?

LILY. Miss Hatfield doesn't understand the time-table for use of kitchen and bathroom that he's drawn up. She's overstepped her time tonight, and he's livid.

ALICE. It sounds very alarming.

LILY. It is. (*She moves to* R *of the table up* LC) Life's one long army manœuvre with the Brigadier. (*Excitedly*) Wait a bit. I think I hear Dame's key. (*She goes into the hall*)

(ALICE *rises and puts her handbag on the table* R.

DAME BEATRICE APPLEBY, D.B.E.—"BEE"—*enters by the front door. She is a woman in late middle age, of tremendous vitality and personality, is a little eccentric in manner and clothes, and has moods that change in a second. At the moment she is very angry*)

BEE (*as she enters; calling*) Lily!
LILY. Evening, Dame dear. Have you had a nice day?
BEE (*coming into the room*) Don't talk to me.

(LILY *follows Bee into the room and takes her hat, coat, gloves and handbag*)

I'm in a filthy temper. Fetch me the medicinal brandy, quickly.
LILY. Dame dear, Lady Miller . . .
BEE. And give me a cushion: I must lie flat on the floor.
LILY. Dame dear . . . (*She gets a cushion from the tub chair* LC *and hands it to Bee*)
BEE (*taking no notice of her*) Thousands of pounds that wretched charity has in the bank. But can I get them to distribute it? (*She waves the cushion*) I might as well try to give the feathers in here back to the birds they came from. (*She puts the cushion on the animal's head of the rug and is about to lie down when she sees Alice*) Alice, my dear! (*To Lily*) Why on earth didn't you tell me?

(ALICE *and* BEE *embrace.*

LILY *shrugs and exits down* L, *taking Bee's hat, coat, gloves and handbag with her*)

(*She draws back from Alice, in horror*) But it can't be you.
ALICE (*apologetically*) It is, darling.
BEE. But you're at Le Touquet making our fortune at roulette.
ALICE. Darling, prepare yourself for a horrible shock.
BEE. Oh, no!
ALICE. Every single penny they got from me.
BEE. All those extra francs I found in my passport, as well?
ALICE. All yours, all mine, and another hundred thousand I raised on my pearls.

(LILY *enters down* L, *crosses to the cabinet up* LC *and takes out a brandy glass.* BEE *lies on the rug with her head on the cushion*)

BEE. Lily, make it a *large* dose of medicinal brandy.
ALICE. Darling, I'm suffering from shock, too. (*She sits on the ottoman at the right end*)
BEE. My dear, I'm so sorry; the disappointment's clouded my brain. Two large doses, Lily.

(LILY *takes a second glass from the cabinet*)

Oh, Alice, I had such schemes for the thousands I was certain you'd win.

ALICE. I'm sure.

BEE. Starting with a party——

(LILY *puts the glasses on the table up* LC *then exits to the hall, closing the doors behind her*)

—where we were going to give our friends little *objets d'art* wrapped up in five-pound notes.

ALICE. If only you'd use that fertile imagination to think of ways of getting money rather than how to give it away.

BEE. But I like giving it away. It's fun. (*She is suddenly gloomy*) Though now I suppose I shall have to dodge even the flag-sellers in the streets on charity days.

ALICE. Rubbish! With all these "lodgers" you must be making a fortune.

BEE. They just enable me to keep abreast of the continual risings in rent. (*She groans, rises and puts the cushion on the ottoman*) But, oh, the misery of being a landlady. The new lodger's already upset Bertie, isn't on speaking terms with Miss Parry, and now wants a new electric stove in her room. (*She crosses to the stove*) While I have to make do with this wretched thing. (*She takes hold of the raker and rattles it furiously in the stove*) What's the matter with it; it's hardly giving out any heat. Wants the sweep, I suppose. Oh, how depressing everything is.

(LILY *enters from the hall carrying a bottle of brandy, which she puts on the table up* LC)

(*Suddenly gay again*) I know what we'll have to cheer us up: champagne!

ALICE. Darling!

BEE (*crossing above the ottoman to* L *of it*) I feel just in the mood for it. Leave that, Lily, and fetch that bottle of champagne I won at the hoop-la.

(LILY *moves to the double doors*)

(*She shivers*) And bring my old fur cape from the hall cupboard.

LILY. Right you are. If I can get it away from the moths.

(LILY *exits to the hall, closing the doors behind her*)

BEE (*gaily*) We must think of some *other* way of making a fortune, Alice.

ALICE (*apprehensively*) Oh, no, don't let's!

BEE. We must have some interest to keep us—(*she flutters her hands*) vibrating. Otherwise, before we know where we are, we shall be in a rut.

ALICE. Darling, you're mad.

BEE. I'm not. These lodgers of mine are a horribly illuminating lesson. (*Going to the cabinet up* LC) They're all dears, really, but because they're in a rut they've become petty and silly, and spend their time quarrelling about nothing. (*She takes two champagne glasses from the cabinet*)

ALICE. It's not so easy to find interests when one's getting towards—the teatime of life.

BEE (*gaily*) Nonsense! (*She shuts the cabinet and moves up* L *of the ottoman*) One can be young at a hundred. (*Angrily*) Not that the nitwits on my committees believe that. Two grey hairs and a wrinkle and one's considered a senile idiot. I'm blessed if the hospital lot didn't suggest that I stop ferrying patients about in my car.

ALICE. It is rather a death-chariot, darling.

BEE (*indignantly*) It's nothing of the sort! It's a dear old car. But the reason they gave was that it was an activity "better left to younger folks". Nincompoops! If I could find the money I'd buy a Jaguar. (*She puts the glasses on the table behind the ottoman*)

ALICE. Pray God you don't!

BEE (*wandering to* L *of the ottoman*) Our experience of life is of immense value, Alice.

ALICE. Of course it is, darling.

BEE (*kneeling on the left end of the ottoman*) We've learnt patience, understanding, tact—(*with a sly smile*) guile—we could do anything if we made up our minds! (*Wickedly*) Let's show them by doing something spectacular.

ALICE (*warily*) Such as?

BEE. Be quiet while I think. (*She crosses down* L)

ALICE (*slowly*) I've been thinking while I've been away. (*She looks sideways at Bee*) What about getting married again?

BEE (*after the slightest pause*) You, or me?

ALICE. Well, I was thinking of me, actually.

BEE (*enthusiastically*) A splendid idea! Why didn't *I* ever think of it? (*She crosses and sits* L *of Alice on the ottoman*) I suppose because you've tried it twice before.

(ALICE *glances sharply at Bee*)

But why not a third time? A wonderful idea. We'll have a quiet, gracious wedding at St Peter's, Eaton Square . . .

ALICE (*laughing*) Now, wait a minute, darling. I have to find a husband first.

BEE. Have you any "possibles"?

ALICE. Well—I've been wondering about your lodger?

BEE (*surprised*) Bertie?

ALICE (*nodding*) Bertie.

BEE (*not pleased*) Oh. (*She rises and crosses to the tub chair* LC)

ALICE. Don't you like the idea?

BEE. I don't think he's very suitable—for *you*. (*She sits in the tub chair*)

ALICE. Oh, I know he's become a bit cranky . . .
BEE. A bit? He now has a patent clock with which he "times" everything. It goes "ping" just at the most awkward moments. Maddening.
ALICE (*rising and crossing to* R *of Bee*) But think what fun he was when we all lived on the Riviera.
BEE (*musingly*) Yes; he was indeed.
ALICE. So witty, and smart. I used to think that you were smitten with him, and was overjoyed when you chose Leo and went off to Hong Kong.
BEE (*meaningly*) Bertie's very different nowadays.
ALICE. If he's changed one way, he can change the other. (*More to herself*) I think I could manage it. He was always prone to flattery. That and talk of the old days . . .

(LILY *enters from the hall. She carries a tray with a bottle of Veuve Cliquot, and a napkin, and also has a fur cape rolled up, inside out, and tucked under her arm. She is bottling up her excitement*)

LILY (*closing the doors*) Here's the grape juice. (*She puts the tray on the table behind the ottoman*)
BEE. Thank you, Lily.
LILY (*moving to* R *of Alice*) Er . . . My lady?
ALICE. Yes?
LILY. Dame's had a lovely nylon jumper sent to her by her niece in Washington. It's in the top drawer of the whatnot in her bedroom. Would you like to go and have a look at it?
BEE. What?
ALICE. Are you trying to get rid of me, Lily?
LILY (*coaxingly*) Just for a tiny minute; do you mind?
ALICE (*crossing to the door down* L) I shall be so tormented as to why I've got to go, that I shan't enjoy the nylon in the slightest. I warn you I'm not going to have a long look.

(ALICE *exits down* L)

BEE. Whatever is all this, Lily?
LILY (*moving behind Bee*) I just didn't want her here when I gave you your fur.
BEE. Why ever not?
LILY. I just didn't, that's all. (*She puts the cape around Bee's shoulders*) There you are. (*She moves to the double doors*)
BEE. Thank you. (*She watches Lily then looks down at the fur*) Lily, one moment! This isn't *my* fur.
LILY (*stopping and turning and pretending astonishment*) Isn't it, Dame, dear?
BEE (*examining the fur*) No. It's . . . (*Amazed*) Why, this is quite beautiful. It looks like mink.
LILY (*moving to* L *of Bee*) It is mink. A first quality "Breath of Spring" mink.

BEE (*puzzled*) "Breath of Spring" mink? But I don't possess anything like this.
LILY. You do *now*.
BEE. I don't understand. (*Becoming alarmed*) Where has it come from?
LILY. Never mind *where*, Dame dear. Just be glad it's *come*.
BEE. What on earth do you mean? Wait a moment. I've seen this before somewhere. These tails. I remember wondering whether they were really the tails belonging to the animals. Now where . . . ? (*Horrified*) Good Heavens! This belongs to the stockbroker's wife in the flat next door, doesn't it?
LILY. Well, let's say it did. (*She crosses below Bee on her way to the double doors*) I'll tell you all about it on a nice rainy afternoon.
BEE (*catching Lily by the hand*) You'll tell me all about it this very moment. It's Mrs Spanager's, isn't it?
LILY (*making for the double doors*) Gracious, I think I've left something in the oven.
BEE. It can stay there. (*Severely*) Now, Lily, I want a full and truthful explanation.
LILY (*moving to* R *of Bee*) Well—(*in a rush*) it was a moment of temptation I succumbed to. I never thought of the ins and outs; just of how you've always longed for a nice fur.
BEE. You mean . . . ?
LILY (*quickly, holding up her hand*) No, wait till you hear, Dame dear! It was "Providence". As I was taking your old mothy out of the cupboard, one of the boozers from next door rang our bell in mistake for the lift. I sent him off with a flea in his ear. Then I noticed that he'd left the Spanagers' front door open, and there on a chest was that mink—smiling up invitingly.
BEE (*ominously*) Go on.
LILY. Well, I've always *longed* to give you a really smashing present to make up for all you've done for me . . .
BEE. I've told you repeatedly that I don't want presents from you.
LILY (*shouting in her effort to explain*) But I wanted to give you one! Working the fingerprints off my fingers isn't enough for all your goodness. You were the only one who'd give me a break when I came out of Holloway.
BEE. It made no difference to me that—your last post was with Her Majesty.
LILY (*kneeling* R *of Bee*) But it did to me. (*Urgently*) And I've always been determined to repay you. (*Dramatically*) And there, suddenly, on that chest, was the answer to the maid's prayer.
BEE. But you promised me you'd never take anything again.
LILY. You know, the thought of you saying that flashed into my mind as I stooped to pick it up. But then I had a bigger flash.
BEE. Pity it wasn't the word "police".

LILY. I saw, as if he was hanging in front of me, a preacher.
BEE. A "preacher"?
LILY. Heard him in Wales, by mistake. His words came ringing back to me: "Those that have two coats should give unto their neighbour one." (*Triumphantly*) What do you think of that?
BEE. I don't see that it has anything to do with it.
LILY (*rising and moving* R) Of course it has. Old Mrs Spanager's got a whole cupboard full. And you're the neighbour with only old mothy.
BEE (*after a slight pause*) Well—(*she removes the cape*) now you'll go straight back, and return it.
LILY. Don't you like it?
BEE (*severely*) Whether I like it or not has nothing to do with it. As you very well know. (*She tosses the cape to Lily*) Here you are.
LILY (*catching the cape*) Well, I'm horrified! After all my trouble. Anyway, how can I take it back? The party's over. I can't hardly ring the bell and say "Here's the fur I pinched five minutes ago."
BEE. No. You can't actually do that. But . . . (*She stops, not knowing what to say*)

(*There is a tap at the double doors.*
    Miss ELIZABETH HATFIELD *enters from the hall. She is small, thin, nervous, untidy and birdlike, and of indeterminate age. She wears a flowered overall heavily smeared with paint marks, and carries a Rockingham teapot covered with strips of brown paper. She is almost in tears of anger*)

HATTIE (*crossing to* L *of Bee*) I'm sorry to disturb you, Dame Beatrice, but I must see you most urgently.
BEE. I'm afraid it isn't very convenient, Miss Hatfield.
LILY (*brightly*) Oh, don't mind me, Dame dear—(*she crosses to Bee*) I was just going, anyhow.

(LILY *quickly puts the cape around Bee's shoulders, and darts out by the double doors*)

BEE. Lily . . . (*She rises to follow Lily*)

(*The* BRIGADIER *enters from the hall. He now wears a butcher's striped apron, and carries his patent pinger.* BEE *resumes her seat in the tub chair*)

HATTIE. The Brigadier's completely ruined one of my client's Rockingham teapots, Dame Beatrice.
BRIGADIER (*moving down* C; *angrily*) I merely turned up the oven to heat through my macaroni cheese.
HATTIE. And made it far too hot for the china I had baking. (*She pokes the teapot at Bee*) Look at the scorches along my joins.
BRIGADIER. Your china-mending shouldn't have been in my oven.

(NAN *enters from the hall, closing the doors behind her*)
The kitchen's mine until nineteen thirty hours. There were still a good ten minutes to go when I came in. (*He shows his pinger*) I set my pinger to ping at nineteen twenty-nine. To give me a minute's warning before my time elapsed. And it hasn't gone off yet.

(*The pinger suddenly emits a loud ping*)
See?

HATTIE. But china-mending is my living, and I do feel...

NAN (*moving to* R *of Bee*) If you've quite finished, Miss Hatfield...

HATTIE (*turning her head from Nan and moving* L) I'm not on speaking terms with you. (*She sits on the desk chair and puts the teapot on the desk*)

NAN (*to the Brigadier*) May I ask you not to hammer on the door when I'm having my bath in the morning, Brigadier?

BRIGADIER. O-seven-thirty hours is my scheduled bath time. It was o-seven-thirty-four when I tapped.

NAN. Tapped! The whole room shook. I was smothered in a shower of rust from the geyser.

BRIGADIER. As Field-Marshal Montgomery said: "Discipline underlies civil life in the same way that it is the basis of military life."

NAN. I bet the poor beast has a nice soak in his bath without Armageddon breaking out. (*She moves below the table up* L)

(ALICE *enters down* L)

ALICE. Am I allowed back yet?

BEE (*rising and crossing to the fireplace*) Come in, Alice, and join the happy throng. You don't know Miss Hatfield. Lady Miller.

ALICE. How do you do?

HATTIE. How do you do?

ALICE (*crossing to* L *of the Brigadier; cooingly*) And, Bertie! What a lovely surprise. You never come and see me, you bad man.

BRIGADIER (*bowing, and kissing Alice's hand*) My dear, you change hotels so frequently that I never know where you are.

ALICE. Well, take my address now—(*she crosses below the ottoman towards her handbag on the table* R) and we'll arrange... (*She breaks off as she sees the fur around Bee's shoulders*) Bee, darling! What a magnificent fur.

BEE (*swallowing*) Yes. Isn't it?

NAN (*moving* L *of the tub chair; suddenly*) Great Scott! It's Mrs Spanager's.

BRIGADIER. Mrs Spanager's? How do you know?

NAN. I've stood next to it in the lift. She explained about the name and colour, and how she'd had the tails made detachable.

BRIGADIER. Are those tails detachable?

(BEE, *in answer, sadly pulls off one of the sets of tails.* HATTIE *rises*)

ALICE. But if it's Mrs Spanager's what are you doing with it?
BEE. Well—er—Lily made a sort of mistake. (*She refixes the tails*)
NAN. Mistake? (*Realizing*) Christmas!
ALICE. You mean that Lily's—reverted?
BEE. Just very temporarily.
BRIGADIER (*appalled*) No!
HATTIE. Has she actually . . . ? (*She makes a "removing" gesture*)

(BEE *nods*)

But how terrible!
BRIGADIER. I warned you against employing a jailbird.
BEE (*angrily*) So you've been proved right—how does that help us?
ALICE. But you mustn't just stand there with it, Bee.
NAN. No, they might think one of us had—taken it.
BEE. It would be very awkward for me to return it. You see, about a week ago when I met Mrs Spanager wearing it, I said, "For two pins I'd steal that."
BRIGADIER. Then what are you going to do, Beatrice?
BEE (*putting the fur on the firestool*) Don't be so infuriating; if I knew, I'd be doing it.
NAN (*to Hattie*) Could one of us return it saying it had been taken in error?
HATTIE (*turning her head away, and crossing below Nan to* L *of Alice*) Perhaps you'd ask Miss Parry, Dame Beatrice, what sort of error there could have been when none of us went to the party.
BRIGADIER. No, no. You must summon Lily, and order her to return it.
BEE (*crossing to* R *of the Brigadier*) She wouldn't even answer the bell in the mood she's in. I know her.
NAN. But she must take it back; there are no two ways about it.
BEE. The Spanagers know about her past. Also she called Mrs Spanager something—appropriate, but not very flattering. If they find out, it'll mean jail for her again. (*She wanders up* R)
HATTIE. Oh, we can't allow that.
NAN. No, I suppose not.
BRIGADIER. No.
ALICE. Certainly not. We must think of some sort of *mistake* to explain it away. Now what? (*She sits in the armchair down* R)
BRIGADIER. Exactly; what?

(BEE *moves to the fire-stool, transfers the fur to the ottoman, then sits on the ottoman at the right end. The* BRIGADIER *puts his pinger on the table up* L, *then sits on the ottoman at the left end.*

NAN *sits in the tub chair.* HATTIE, *after dithering, sits on the animal head. They think in silence for a moment*)

NAN (*suddenly*) Could we throw it back from the pantry window?

BRIGADIER. Quite impracticable.

NAN. A really good shot ought to be able to get it into their window opposite. I used to be a dab at a coconut shy.

BRIGADIER. This isn't a coconut. It's a cape.

BEE. Besides, that's their kitchen window. If it sailed on to the stove we should be liable for arson as well as theft.

HATTIE (*horrified*) Oh, please don't use the word "theft".

BRIGADIER. It's the word that'll be used if we're discovered in a guilty circle round it.

(HATTIE *rises in horror and moves to the table up* L. BEE *throws the fur on to the fire-stool*)

(*He rises*) We're being weak-minded. (*He crosses to the desk*) There's only one correct line of action; ring up the police.

HATTIE (*very alarmed*) Oh, no, no, no!

NAN }
BEE } (*together*) No!

BRIGADIER. Why not?

HATTIE (*moving to* R *of the Brigadier*) The police would never believe I'd just "forgotten" to get a wireless licence.

NAN. I'd owe a fortune to the income-tax if they found out about my pupils.

BEE (*thoughtfully*) I've never actually declared your rents. No, wiser not to have the police.

ALICE. Unless they arrive on their own.

HATTIE. Oh, don't! (*Agitatedly*) There must be something we can do.

(*There is a pause while they ponder*)

NAN. Got it! Post it back anonymously. I can disguise the address for the label. I could copy any of the girls' handwriting at school.

HATTIE (*turning her head away from Nan*) Perhaps you'd remind Miss Parry, Brigadier, that the post office is closed.

NAN. Curse!

ALICE. You daren't have it in the flat till the morning.

BEE. We're getting warmer, though. Think hard again, everyone.

(*They all think. The* BRIGADIER *wanders up* C)

NAN. It's a real teaser.

BEE (*suddenly*) I think I have it.

BRIGADIER (*moving to* L *of the ottoman*) How?

B

BEE. One of us must slip back with it under cover of some sort of "created confusion".

(*The others look puzzled*)

ALICE. Could you be the weeist bit more explicit, darling?

BEE. We must arrange—a set of circumstances, so that we get the Spanagers' front door open, with them occupied somewhere else.

BRIGADIER (*thoughtfully*) Possible, possible. (*Enthusiastically*) But if we're to consider plans, we must draw up a proper tactical appreciation based on the military formula.

HATTIE. Oh, dear, must we?

BRIGADIER (*severely*) Yes. We must.

(HATTIE *moves above the table up* L)

(*He removes his apron*) It ensures that no point is overlooked. Now, Beatrice, have you a large sheet of paper?

BEE (*rising*) What about the back of these cards? (*She takes some invitation cards from the mantelpiece and hands them to the Brigadier*)

BRIGADIER (*enjoying himself*) Capital! (*He crosses to* L, *throws his apron on to the chair below the table up* L, *then sits at the desk*) Now, let me see—what were the approved military headings? (*He mumbles to himself and writes*) "Information", "Intention", er . . .

BEE. How can we get the Spanagers out of their flat for a vital moment?

NAN (*delightedly*) A fire! That's it. Set something alight in the passage, and then shout "Fire!" through their letter-box.

HATTIE (*moving to* R *of Nan*) Oh, surely we needn't have a real fire. Oh! Now I've spoken to you. Well—owing to the emergency I'll suspend my ban.

BEE. Thank heaven!

ALICE (*rising*) The lift! That's the solution.

BRIGADIER. What do you mean, my dear?

ALICE (*crossing excitedly to the Brigadier*) Well, it's prehistoric. What more natural than that it should break down, and one of us be trapped?

HATTIE (*excitedly*) Good, good. Stop it between floors, by opening the gate a bit, and then scream.

NAN. All that would happen is the rude porter would arrive.

BEE (*moving behind the tub chair*) We must dispose of the porter, then.

HATTIE (*horrified*) Dame Beatrice!

BEE. I don't mean "bump him off". (*After a moment's thought*) We could send him on an errand.

BRIGADIER (*delightedly jotting it down*) "To fetch a taxi for Alice." He's done that often.

ALICE. Excellent! They're always impossible to get round here at this time of night.

BEE. Now, who shall be the one . . . ?
BRIGADIER (*interrupting determinedly*) We'll take the points *in order*, if you please. Now—*number of enemy?*
NAN. Mr and Mrs Spanager, and his old mother—Madame Spanager.
HATTIE. Oh, bother. We'll never get her out of the flat.
NAN. No, she's practically gaga.
ALICE. So long as she's too far gone to move from her room, we're all right.
BEE. She's not so far gone that she mightn't ring up the police when she hears the screams.
BRIGADIER (*noting it down*) The telephone must be made unavailable. Beatrice, you will ring her up at the vital time.
BEE. To say what? I hardly know her.
NAN. Pretend you're interested in buying one of those knitting machines she's so potty about.
BEE. I don't know anything about knitting. The bed-jacket I made had to be turned into a hot-water bottle cover.
HATTIE. Wait a moment. I know.

(HATTIE *rushes out by the double doors*)

ALICE. What does she know?
BRIGADIER (*furious*) It's most irregular to leave a conference like that. Number of enemy, then: three. No possible *reinforcements?*
BEE. No. Their daily will have left, and they won't be having the Hungarian who cooks dinners; they'll be eating party leftovers.

(HATTIE *runs back from the hall, closing the doors behind her. She carries a crumpled sheet of the "Radio Times"*)

HATTIE (*moving to R of the tub chair*) Here you are, the very thing. A broken china elephant arrived in it. (*She hands the sheet to Bee and points to an advertisement*) That advertisement tells you all about knitting machines.
BEE (*studying the advertisement*) If Madame Spanager understands this she's not as gaga as she makes out.
BRIGADIER (*looking up from his "orders"*) Which of you *screams* the loudest?
BEE. Nan. All that voice production.
NAN (*rising, crossing and standing above the desk*) Yes, I think I can guarantee that the poor beasts will run out when they hear me.
BEE. Mrs Spanager will just dither about, but he's very energetic. He may be down and up the stairs again before we have time to replace the fur.
BRIGADIER. An *obstacle* must be put in his way. What?

(*They all think*)

HATTIE (*suddenly*) Me!
BEE. I doubt whether you'd be a big enough obstacle, dear.
HATTIE. As Mr Spanager passes, I'll faint into his arms. That'd be a nice obstacle, wouldn't it?
BRIGADIER (*writing*) Good. Obstacle: Miss Hatfield. The plan's shaping.

(*There is a sudden knock at the double doors. The planners are paralyzed*)

HATTIE (*panic-stricken*) The Spanagers! (*She crosses to* R, *seizes the fur, dithers, eventually hides it in the armchair down* R *and sits on it*)

(BEE *takes* NAN'S *arm, crosses with her to* R *of the ottoman, then sits on the ottoman and tucks the sheet of the "Radio Times" under the cushion.* NAN *sits on the fire-stool.* ALICE *sits on the chair below the table up* L. *The* BRIGADIER *remains in his chair at the desk*)

BEE (*calling*) Come in.

(LILY *enters from the hall. She carries a bowl of salad*)

... so they pulled the strings of their parachutes, and landed in a potato field.

(*After a moment of blankness, they all join in forced comment and laughter.* LILY *puts the salad on the table up* L)

LILY (*moving* C *and clapping her hands and speaking like a barmaid*) Come along, time, please. Time, please. All out. I want to give Dame her dinner.

(*There is a pause as the others all look at* LILY)

BEE. I'm—I'm not very hungry, Lily. Postpone the meal half an hour, will you?
LILY. Right you are. (*She moves up* C, *sees them all looking at her, stops, and exaggeratedly examines her dress*) What's the matter? Is my slip showing?
BEE. They've found out, Lily.
LILY. Oh! I thought I felt something in the air. (*She looks at the Brigadier*) It must be all the "I-told-you-so's" flying about.
HATTIE. It's terrible, Lily.
LILY (*gaily*) No, it's not. You don't have to worry that Mrs Spanager will recognize it, you know. By the time I've finished with it the bloke who made it wouldn't swear to it.
ALICE (*rising and moving to* L *of Lily*) You know about furs?
LILY. What do you think I was in Holloway for?
ALICE (*sitting in the tub chair*) Oh, my dear!
LILY. I worked as a machinist in a place that made fur coats. That's what led to me downfall. (*Professionally*) I'll take off the tails, check identification marks on the skins, remodel the style a little, and put in a new lining.

(*They all gasp*)
Or have you other plans?

(*They all start denying this at once*)

(*She exaggeratedly covers her ears*) No, no, no! Don't tell me. I have an idea it would be a petty falsehood. And if there's one thing that appals me it's a petty falsehood. (*She moves to the double doors and turns*) No. If you have to get round something, tell an absolute whopper, and waltz round in style. (*She moves down* C *and looks around at the others*) Has that penetrated through the soil to the roots? Because it's useful information in case anyone comes round enquiring about—the mantle that's fallen from Heaven. Agree on your whopper, and stick to it. (*She moves to the double doors and opens them*) And if you want to hide it temporarily, for Gawd's sake do it better than that.

(LILY *nods towards the armchair down* R *and exits to the hall closing the doors behind her.* HATTIE *grabs the end of the fur which has been sticking out, and tucks it under her*)

ALICE (*in a low voice, looking at the doors*) If we're not careful there's going to be a large fly in our ointment.

BEE (*rising and crossing to the table up* L) We must get her out of the way.

BRIGADIER. What would be a plausible excuse for sending her out at this time of night?

(*They all ponder*)

HATTIE (*suddenly*) Senna pods?
BRIGADIER (*shocked*) Miss Hatfield! Please!
ALICE (*rising and standing* R *of Bee*) What about that boy-friend of hers? Couldn't you give her the evening off?
BEE (*looking at her watch*) He's just been made fireman on the night ferry. He'll be on duty by now.
ALICE. Can't life be perverse? (*She crosses and sits on the left end of the ottoman*)
BEE (*clapping her hands*) Sleeping pills! Mrs Roberts in the next block has just been abroad and has smuggled in some very potent ones. (*She moves to the desk*) Out of the way, Bertie.

(*The* BRIGADIER *rises*)

(*She sits at the desk, lifts the telephone receiver and dials a number*) I'll give her a ring, and Lily can go and collect them.

NAN (*rising, crossing and standing above the tub chair*) We must be jolly careful she doesn't use the lift when we want it.

BRIGADIER. Yes; the timing of each phase of the attack will be critical. Don't worry, I'm working on it. (*He sits on the chair below the table up* L)

BEE (*into the telephone*) Ivy? . . . Beatrice . . . You know those sleeping pills? . . . Could I borrow one tonight? . . . Thank you so much, dear. I'll send Lilly straight away . . . Oh, and while she's there do show her that coffee percolator . . . Yes . . . Thank you so much, dear . . . Good-bye. (*She replaces the receiver*) A most complicated paraphernalia. Lily'll be there hours.

BRIGADIER. Splendid! (*He rises*) Then this is the plan I propose. Pay careful attention, please. (*He picks up his pinger and shows it*) I set the pinger, and when it pings, the first wave goes in.

HATTIE (*rising*) Please don't be so military, Brigadier. It conjures up the most frightful visions. (*She resumes her seat*)

BRIGADIER. Two minutes before that, you, Beatrice, will despatch Lily Thompson on pill expedition. (*He puts the pinger on the table up* L)

BEE. She'll be difficult.

BRIGADIER. You must overcome that. On hearing pinger, Alice and Miss Parry will descend in lift. At ground level, the first-mentioned will despatch porter, and then hold herself in readiness to waylay enemy reinforcements.

ALICE. If anyone comes I'll drop pennies about. I did it once when I *had* to get on a bus and there was a long queue. It worked wonders.

BRIGADIER. Miss Parry will in the meantime *ascend* in lift, and take the planned action at a suitable elevation.

NAN. Open the gate, and scream. Yes. (*She moves above the ottoman*)

BRIGADIER (*moving to* R *of Bee*) Up here, Beatrice will engage Madame Spanager on the telephone.

BEE. If she lands me with one of those knitting machines, you'll pay for it.

BRIGADIER (*crossing below the ottoman*) On hearing screams, Miss Hatfield will leave base, proceed to Spanager door, and cause general alarm.

HATTIE. But I thought I was to . . .

BRIGADIER (*fiercely*) No interruptions, if you please. She will then retreat to lift, and prepare to ambush Mr Spanager. Understood?

HATTIE. I think so.

BRIGADIER (*severely*) Not good enough; you must be sure.

HATTIE. Oh, dear! Then I'm as sure as I'll ever be.

BRIGADIER. I suppose we shall have to be satisfied with that. (*He moves above the tub chair*) *I* shall be holding myself in readiness, and under cover of resulting confusion, shall infiltrate into stronghold and *replace object.*

ALICE (*rising and moving to* R *of the Brigadier*) Wonderful, Bertie! I'd no idea you were such a brilliant planner. Seeing you standing there so confidently reminds me . . .

BEE (*interrupting firmly, rising and moving to* L *of the Brigadier*) Let's have your reminiscences later, Alice. (*To the Brigadier;*

winningly) Though I must say, Bertie—it's a miracle of a plan.
NAN. Can't fail. Touch wood. (*She touches the table above the ottoman*)
BRIGADIER (*delighted*) Thank you, thank you. Now, any questions?
BEE. How exactly are we to know when the battle is over?
NAN. Yes. We ought to have a signal when it's safe to pull up stumps.
HATTIE (*rising and rushing out of the double doors*) I know!

(HATTIE *exits to the hall.* NAN *moves up* RC)

BRIGADIER (*annoyed*) I fear Miss Hatfield little understands the word "discipline".
BEE (*crossing to the table above the ottoman*) It's only nerves, Bertie. I don't feel so calm myself. (*She indicates the champagne*) Could the troops partake of a little something before going over the top?
BRIGADIER. In moderation, an excellent idea. (*He crosses to* L *of Bee, picks up the champagne bottle and opens it*)

(BEE *goes to the cabinet up* LC, *collects three champagne glasses and puts them on the table behind the ottoman.*

HATTIE *enters up* C, *blowing a whistle which has a white tape attached. She closes the doors*)

(*Annoyed*) Miss Hatfield! (*He crosses to Hattie*)
HATTIE. Here we are. The whistle I keep by my bedside in case of burglars. (*She puts he whistle around the Brigadier's neck*)
ALICE. My dear, how wise. (*To the Brigadier*) Give a long blast when it's safe to relax.
BRIGADIER. Agreed. (*He goes to the table and gives the bottle of champagne to Bee*) And in case of emergency I'll give a series of short, sharp blasts.
NAN. What do we do, then?
BRIGADIER (*after a moment's hesitation*) Act spontaneously. Now, any final questions?
BEE (*pouring the champagne*) There can't be, I'm issuing the rum ration. Help yourselves, everyone.

(*The* BRIGADIER *picks up two glasses and holds one out to Hattie*)

HÁTTIE. Oh, my goodness, not for me. (*She takes the glass and passes it to Alice*)
NAN (*moving above the left end of the ottoman*) Don't be a juggins; it'll do you good. (*She takes a glass for herself*)
HATTIE. I'd be sick. (*She crosses and sits in the tub chair*) Unfortunately, I've run out of my nerve tonic, or I'd have a good spoon of that.
BRIGADIER (*starting a speech*) Before we embark on this—I must admit—precarious adventure, I feel it both my duty and my honour . . .

BEE (*picking up her glass*) No, no, not now, Bertie. When we're safely back in camp. (*She raises her glass*) Good luck to us all.

(BEE, NAN, *the* BRIGADIER *and* ALICE *clink their glasses together with murmured salutations, drink, then put their glasses on the table behind the ottoman*)

BRIGADIER. I'll wind the pinger. (*He crosses to the table up* L *and winds the pinger*)

(ALICE *crosses to* R *of the Brigadier*)

Now, is everyone ready?

HATTIE. One moment! (*She rises*) I don't think I am. (*She rushes to the double doors*)

BEE (*intercepting Hattie*) Yes, yes, you are. (*In a low voice*) It's only going to take five minutes.

HATTIE (L *of Bee; doubtfully*) Oh. All right.

BRIGADIER. Then—(*he sets the pinger on the table up* L) we're off. I've set it two minutes to starting time. Beatrice—Lily Thompson.

BEE. Mercy on me! (*She crosses bravely and presses the bell-push above the fireplace*)

(*The others turn and stare expectantly at the double doors*)

Don't all be staring. Behave naturally. (*She sits on the right arm of the ottoman and takes some embroidery from her workbag*)

(ALICE *crosses and sits on the left end of the ottoman. The* BRIGADIER, HATTIE *and* NAN *make for the tub chair and collide.* NAN *sits in the tub chair. The* BRIGADIER *crosses down* R, *takes a paper from the newspaper rack and stands reading by the stove.* HATTIE *goes to the window, picks up a watering-can and crosses to the plant-table below the screen. There is a pause*)

HATTIE. Why doesn't she come?

(NAN *rises, crosses down* R, *picks up the fur and drapes it over Bee's shoulders*)

NAN. Better drape yourself in the mink to put her off the scent. (*She sits in the armchair down* R)

BRIGADIER. First-class smoke screen.

(*They wait*)

HATTIE. What on earth's she doing? She'll ruin the whole thing. (*She hastens to the double doors, opens them and calls*) Li-ly!

(LILY *enters almost immediately from the hall*)

LILY. *Ye-es?*

(HATTIE *darts away to the window and replaces the watering-can*)

(*She looks around*) Hullo, hullo! Still chewing the cud?

BEE. Lily, dear—(*she swallows*) I want you to fetch some sleeping pills from Mrs Roberts. I've rung her, and she's waiting. Will you do that?

(LILY *gazes at them for a moment*)

LILY (*cheerfully*) Right you are—won't be two shakes of a lamb's tail.

(LILY *smiles at them and exits immediately to the hall, closing the doors behind her. The others are suitably amazed*)

NAN. There must be something the matter with the poor beast.

BEE. It's a splendid omen. (*She removes the fur and puts it* R *of her on the ottoman*)

ALICE. Or alarmingly suspicious.

(*The telephone rings. They all gasp, especially* HATTIE)

BEE. But we never planned for anyone to ring *us* up. What shall I do?

ALICE. Don't answer.

HATTIE. If it's a talker you'll never get on to Madame Spanager.

BEE. But—oh, I don't know what to do. Bertie?

(*The telephone stops ringing*)

Heaven be praised!

HATTIE. I hope it wasn't something important.

(*The pinger rings loudly*)

(*She screams sharply*) Aah!

NAN. What the blazes, Hattie! I'm the screamer.

HATTIE. I'm so sorry. (*She crosses above the ottoman to* R *of it*) Oh, my heart's beating as if I'd run the hundred yards.

BRIGADIER (*crossing to the table up* L) Come along—come along! No dilly-dallying. (*Ordering*) The *first wave*.

(*No-one reacts*)

(*He shouts*) The first wave.

ALICE (*rising*) That's us. Come on, Miss Parry.

(ALICE *exits to the hall and collects her coat.* NAN *rises, crosses towards the hall and stops* C)

NAN (*holding her throat*) My throat's gone dry. I shan't get out a sound.

BEE (*rising*) Yes, you will. Good luck. Good luck.

(NAN *goes into the hall, and exits by the front door.*
During this, HATTIE, *unseen by the audience, slips the fur out of sight behind the coal scuttle.*
ALICE *enters from the hall*)

ALICE. Oh, my dear, how exciting! I feel like a toreador about to tackle his first bull. *Olé!*

(ALICE *waves her coat, taps her heels on the floor, and goes into the hall and exits by the front door*)

BRIGADIER (*consulting his "orders"*) Next? You, Beatrice.

BEE (*in a panic*) No, no, I'm not ready. (*She snatches up the sheet of the "Radio Times"*) I haven't studied the machine yet. Wait a minute.

BRIGADIER (*shouting*) Impossible! You'll upset the whole schedule. Begin!

BEE (*frantically reading as she crosses to the desk*) "Pair of men's socks knitted in forty-five minutes." (*She stands at the desk and lifts the telephone receiver*) Forty-five minutes? (*She dials a number*)

BRIGADIER (*looking at his watch and "orders"*) Miss Hatfield, take up your position in hall.

HATTIE (*without moving*) It's no good. I can't go through with it. I'm too nervous.

BRIGADIER. Think how much more nervous you'd be at the Central Criminal Court.

(HATTIE, *with a gasp of horror, rushes below the ottoman into the hall*)

BEE. Why doesn't she answer? (*She reads*) "Rustless, stitch sinker." What on earth can that be? (*Into the telephone*) Hullo—Madame Spanager? . . .

BRIGADIER (*in a whisper*) Courage.

BEE (*into the telephone*) This is Beatrice Appleby . . . How are you? . . . Not venturing out in this cold weather, I hope? . . . Good . . . (*She nods encouragingly at the Brigadier*)

(*The* BRIGADIER *goes to the front door and peers down the corridor*)

Now, I want the benefit of your experience. I'm thinking of buying an—(*she reads*) "automatic, high-speed, Quiknit home-knitting machine". Would you advise that? . . .

(NAN *is heard off, screaming loud and long.* HATTIE *clasps her hands together in prayer; and the* BRIGADIER *gestures to her.*

HATTIE *exits by the front door. The* BRIGADIER *takes up a position, peering out of the three-quarter closed front door*)

(*She anxiously watches the Brigadier, forgetting the telephone, then suddenly realizes. Into the telephone*) I'm so sorry—I had my attention distracted . . . Tell me, is it true that—(*she reads*) "on sixteen garments I could save seven hundred and fifty-six knitting hours"? . .

HATTIE (*off; calling*) Help, Mr Spanager, help!

BEE (*into the telephone*) Fancy! And is the "steel-reinforced needle-bed" really unbreakable? . . . (*She only half listens as she watches the Brigadier*)

(*The* BRIGADIER *pops his head in and out of the front door. Confused noise and voices are heard. The* BRIGADIER *rushes into the room and looks wildly around*)

BRIGADIER (R *of the tub chair*) Where is it?
BEE (*to the Brigadier*) Where's what?
BRIGADIER (*frantically*) The mink, of course.
BEE. Haven't you got it?
BRIGADIER. No, *you* had it.
BEE. No, I didn't.
BRIGADIER. Of course you did.

(*The* BRIGADIER, *in complete disorder, looks under the armchair down* R, *and behind the ottoman, dashes up* L, *searches behind the curtains and then looks in other unlikely places*)

(*Into the telephone and also searching wildly*) How interesting. And do you find the "lightning latch-opener" satisfactory? . . . (*To the Brigadier*) It must be somewhere. (*She puts the sheet of the "Radio Times" on the tub chair and crawls around, as far as the telephone wire permits, searching for the fur*)

BRIGADIER (*searching frantically*) This is terrible!
BEE. Hattie must have put it out of sight. (*Into the telephone*) Madame Spanager, shall I be able to knit circular articles and curved yokes? . . . (*She spots the fur. To the Brigadier*) There! There, by the coal scuttle.

(*The* BRIGADIER *grabs the fur, rolls it up, puts it under his coat with one end hanging out behind, and rushes out by the front door*)

(*She moves to the desk; into the telephone*) No, no, I'm still here . . . Shall I be able to understand the profusely illustrated brochure? . . . And I must know whether I can do my favourite patterns such as "Fair Isle" and "Fisherman's Rib". Especially "Fisherman's Rib"? . . .

(*The* BRIGADIER *enters by the front door and comes into the room, panting heavily*)

(*To the Brigadier*) Thank goodness! Blow your whistle.

(*The* BRIGADIER *blows the whistle with a dying breath, and collapses, exhausted, on to the ottoman*)

(*Into the telephone*) Get suction-type rubber feet? . . . Oh, yes, I will. But I must go now—my—my bath's running over. (*She hastily replaces the receiver and crosses to the Brigadier*) All well?

BRIGADIER (*mopping his brow and hardly able to speak*) As far as I could see, it went without a hitch. But, oh, my heart! Thumping like a battering ram.

BEE (*pouring a brandy*) A drop of medicinal will steady you. Where did you put it?

BRIGADIER (*rising*) I tucked it between the wall and the chest.

(*He takes the drink from Bee*) With just a tuft sticking out. (*He crosses and sits on the chair below the table up* L)

BEE. Ideal! Clever man!

BRIGADIER. And you, my dear. You might have invented the knitting machine.

(NAN *enters backwards by the front door, supporting the collapsed* HATTIE, *and speaking over her body to the unseen helpers*)

NAN. Quite all right now, thank you. No, don't bother, please. I can manage—she's still a little faint, poor beast. But I can cope. Good night. (*She kicks the front door shut*)

(*The limp* HATTIE *immediately revives. She and* NAN *hurry into the room*)

HATTIE (*standing above the ottoman*) Is it back?

BEE. Beautifully back. And all's safe. That was a magnificent scream, Nan. (*She crosses to* LC)

NAN (*moving to* R *of Bee*) Did you hear it? (*Enthusiastically*) What fun, wasn't it? It all went like clockwork.

BEE (*to the Brigadier; admiringly*) The result of the superb planning.

HATTIE (*to Nan; enthusiastically*) I could have sworn you were really terrified in the lift. Splendid, you were.

NAN (*delighted*) Thank you, dear! (*She puts her arm around Hattie*) But your faint was the highlight. Wonderfully convincing.

HATTIE (*thrilled*) Oh, thank you, Nan. And did you see the Brigadier? He skipped down the passage like a young lamb.

(*There is a sudden ring at the front door. They are all paralyzed for a moment. The ring is repeated*)

NAN (*hurrying to the front door*) It's all right—Lady Miller.

(HATTIE *sits on the ottoman, facing up stage*)

BRIGADIER. Of course—Alice.

(NAN *opens the front door.*
    ALICE *enters by the front door and goes to* L *of Bee*)

ALICE (*out of breath*) Successful?

(NAN *closes the front door, comes into the room and closes the double doors*)

BRIGADIER (*rising and crossing to* C) Remarkably successful.

ALICE (*admiringly*) I knew it would be with your wonderful plan.

BEE (*moving quickly and purposefully between Alice and the Brigadier; to Alice*) Did your part go all right?

ALICE. My dear, the porter's still not back. I demanded an *elderly, safe* cabman.

BEE. Inspiration!

NAN. It was all a triumph. I feel quite exhilarated. (*She crosses down* L, *doing a little dance*) Toll-der-roll-oll.
HATTIE (*rising and moving* R) I haven't *ever* done anything so exciting.
BEE (*moving to the table above the ottoman*) We must celebrate. (*She pours out the remainder of the champagne*) Even you, Hattie. (*She hands a glass to Hattie*)
HATTIE (*crossing with the glass to Nan*) Oh, no, thank you. (*She hands the glass to Nan*)

(ALICE, BEE *and the* BRIGADIER *take their glasses*)

But I'll make a cup of tea when I've calmed down. Oh, bother, it's not my time for the kitchen.
BRIGADIER (*moving to* R *of Hattie; good-humouredly*) We might make an exception this once, dear.
BEE (*moving to* R *of the ottoman*) Let us drink to our victory. To the return of—"The Breath of Spring".

(*They raise their glasses, repeat "The Breath of Spring" and drink*)

ALICE. "The Breath of Spring." It might have blown round me. I feel five years younger.
BEE. I feel ten years younger.

(ALICE *glances sharply at Bee*)

BRIGADIER (*raising his glass*) I drink to the magnificent way you all behaved "under fire", so to speak.
ALICE (*raising her glass to the Brigadier*) We couldn't have done it without your inspiring leadership, Bertie.
BEE (*moving quickly between the Brigadier and Alice*) I felt invulnerable with such an able commander. (*She holds up her glass to the Brigadier*)
ALICE (*to Bee; acidly*) That's what I said, darling.
BRIGADIER (*moving between Alice and Bee; delighted*) You're both very kind.

(NAN *drains her glass and crosses behind the ottoman*)

NAN. Thank you. Very refreshing. (*She puts her glass on the table behind the ottoman, then moves to the double doors. Slowly*) Well, I must go and get out practice lists of rising and falling inflections. What a bore.

(*They are all dispirited.* ALICE *puts her glass on the table behind the ottoman, then crosses to the table* R *and collects her gloves and bag. The* BRIGADIER *puts his glass on the table up* L)

ALICE. I'm late for dinner already. Oh dear, my hotel's going to seem duller than ever tonight.
HATTIE (*collecting her teapot from the desk*) I don't feel at all like my blessed china mending.

BRIGADIER (*collecting his apron and pinger*) I think I'll toddle off to early bed. Our *coup's* rather taken it out of me.

HATTIE (*wistfully*) But what fun it was. (*Eagerly*) I wouldn't mind doing it all over again.

(*They all cheer up again and speak with growing excitement*)

ALICE. Neither would I. It gave me shivers down my back for the first time for ages.

NAN (*moving slightly in from the door*) It was amazing how smoothly it went.

ALICE (*nodding*) We might have "operated" together for years.

BEE (*moving down stage a little, and smiling happily at the memory*) Yes—we prove to be a most accomplished "gang", don't we?

BRIGADIER. Yes, indeed!

BEE. You, Bertie, the planner . . .

BRIGADIER. Miss Parry for simulated voices and dramatic impersonations.

ALICE. You, Bee, with your fertile mind, for ideas . . .

NAN. Hattie, neat-fingered and quick . . .

BEE. And all of us considered beyond even raiding a larder! (*She moves down stage two steps. After the slightest pause*) You know, we must think more about this.

HATTIE (*breathlessly*) What do you mean, Dame Beatrice?

BEE. Well—(*slowly*) surely it's a shameful waste of our talents to use them only for *replacing* furs?

The others gaze at Bee with dawning wonder and excitement, and move towards her as—

the CURTAIN *falls*

ACT II

SCENE—*The same. Six months later. Early afternoon.*
The furniture has been rearranged. The tub chair has been removed, and the table from up L *is now down* LC, *and there are three upright chairs above it, an upright chair* R *of it and the desk chair* L *of it. Each place is set with notebooks with pencils attached, and copies of reports; the Brigadier's clip-board with "orders", a brass handbell, a water carafe and glass are also on the table. The fire-stool is below the table. The screen up* R *is opened, and the ottoman is set more angled to the fireplace. There are bowls and vases of autumn flowers everywhere.*

When the CURTAIN *rises, it is about two o'clock. The stove is lit, and the balcony window is open. The* BRIGADIER, BEE, HATTIE, NAN *and* ALICE *are sitting formally round the table.* NAN *is* L *of it;* BEE *is* R *of Nan; the* BRIGADIER *is* R *of Bee;* ALICE *is* R *of the Brigadier and* HATTIE *is* R *of the table. A great change is immediately obvious. Not only are they all jovial and happy, but they look younger, and are gaily dressed. The* BRIGADIER *is especially spruce and energetic. The* BRIGADIER *rises. The others applaud.*

BRIGADIER. Thank you, thank you. (*With great panache*) As chairman, I should like to open this meeting with a few words concerning this auspicious day which marks our *first half-year in business.*

(*The others applaud gaily*)

In those six months, we have carried out two large-scale, and seven smaller-scale, transactions concerning furs.

(*There are murmurs of appreciation*)

We have seen the great strength that lies in our unusual methods of operation; and where our organization has its weaknesses. (*His eyes rest on Hattie*)
HATTIE (*pushing her chair back*) Oh, I don't think that's fair. It was due to sheer bad luck that I missed that silver fox.
BRIGADIER. Dear Hattie, I assure you I was speaking quite generally. (*He continues his speech*) I fear that business interests have somewhat interfered with your usual occupations . . .
HATTIE (*interrupting*) Oh, I don't mind at all. Yesterday I broke the tail off a Dresden cow, and I didn't feel a qualm.
BEE. I haven't enjoyed myself so much since Leo and I were in Delhi. And I'm so well. My doctor's furious. (*She smiles at the Brigadier*) You look wonderfully well, too, Bertie.

ALICE (*smiling at the Brigadier*) Doesn't he? A picture of health.
BEE. Years younger, too!

(*The* BRIGADIER, *delighted, brushes his moustache as he turns to each.* ALICE *looks at Bee with growing worry, and is determined not to be outbid*)

ALICE. And so full of energy!
BEE (*after an amused glance at her*) Yes, and so handsome!
ALICE (*after glancing at Bee*) And you make the points so clearly in your splendid voice!
BEE. Quite the most admirable chairman!
BRIGADIER (*ringing his bell*) Order, please, order. I conclude this brief peroration by paying tribute to the loyal and ungrudging service given by you all. Continue in the same devoted way, and we may face the future with growing confidence, and sober optimism. (*He resumes his seat*)

(*The others applaud*)

I now call upon our treasurer, Miss Nanette Parry, to review, briefly, the financial events of the half-year.

(NAN *rises and stands above her chair*)

NAN. It won't take a jiffy. From the figures you have in front of you, you'll see that, compared with the quantity of stuff we've dealt with, our receipts are measly.
HATTIE (*looking at her copy of the report*) But there's a nice little sum in the kitty.
NAN. It should be very much more. For instance—it was wicked only getting twenty pounds for that Persian lamb. I saw an identical one in Bond Street priced at three hundred guineas.
ALICE (*shaking her hand*) Our "disposal" arrangements are very unsatisfactory.
HATTIE. Yes, Josh Limes is a rotten fence. He diddles us quite shamefully.
NAN (*thoughtfully*) Lily was inside owing to furs. She'd probably know a better fence.
BEE (*firmly*) No! We must continue to keep Lily in complete ignorance of our—organization.
BRIGADIER. Yes, we agreed on that. Don't worry—(*he makes a note*) I think I can find a new fence through an ex-batman of mine. Any further financial points, Miss Parry?
NAN (*ominously*) One more. We agreed that—as we don't take a penny of profits for ourselves—we should be allowed reasonable expenses such as buses, occasional taxis, light meals while on duty, et cetera, et cetera. But the operative word was "reasonable". (*Severely*) Some items on some expense sheets are becoming decidedly questionable.

BEE. Don't look at me—(*she indicates the room*) I don't even charge office or boardroom rent.
HATTIE. You may think my bottles of nerve-tonic illegitimate. But I only needed one a year before.
NAN. No, they're permissible. Just as much as the Brigadier's occasional double whiskies.

(*The* BRIGADIER *reacts*)

I'm not criticizing; just saying don't let's overdo it. That's all. (*She resumes her seat*)

(*There is short and very unenthusiastic applause*)

BRIGADIER. Dame Beatrice, will you report on "Distribution of Profits"?
BEE (*rising*) I am very happy to announce that yesterday we posted off our *thirty-eighth* parcel of pound notes.

(*The others applaud and comment*)

ALICE. How right they were to make you a Dame for collecting large sums for charity.
BEE. As we have to remain anonymous, it is seldom that we hear of the relief and joy caused by our parcels of money. But in two cases my observations seem to prove the success of our work. Case three—(*they all find it on their lists*) Mr and Mrs "S". They added our money to their tiny savings, and have just come back from ten days in Italy. They look so different; I wish you could see them. They still have sad and difficult days ahead of them, but that holiday, I'm sure, literally saved their lives. Case seventeen—Major "W". He *didn't* buy the winter overcoat as we intended. Instead he hired a television set. But he entertains all the other lonely old things in his boarding-house with it, and now of course doesn't need an overcoat as he never goes out.
HATTIE. Such cases are really very encouraging.
BEE. A special word of thanks is due to Alice, who in her moves from hotel to hotel, in South Kensington and Bayswater, has been so successful in finding the majority of our deserving cases.
ALICE. How kind.
BEE. Finally, please let me have your list of those in want—all sorts—in good time for my next "Distribution" sub-committee. Thank you. (*She resumes her seat*)

(*The others applaud*)

BRIGADIER. Next—"Complaints". Two this time. (*He rises*) First—from Beatrice. She feels that we're not being sufficiently careful about taking *only from those perfectly able to afford it*.
ALICE. It's horribly difficult; people are so deceitful about how much money they've got.

BEE. I don't want to find we've been "unfair" to anybody.

BRIGADIER. Please all bear the point strongly in mind. Next complaint—from Hattie. She's not happy about doing so much "trailing". (*He resumes his seat*)

ALICE (*to Hattie*) It is exhausting. But we've had such useful information by following a good coat, and listening to it in shops.

HATTIE. But hanging about—especially in Piccadilly at dusk— I've had most unpleasant experiences.

NAN. Funny. I never have.

BEE. Then the solution's obvious; Hattie must do the earlier hours, and Nan the later.

(NAN *takes a moment to realize the implication, then reacts*)

BRIGADIER (*making a note*) I'll bear it in mind when drawing up the duty rosters. Now—"Suggestions". Miss Hatfield?

HATTIE (*rising*) Just one, from Nan. She asks us to sanction the purchase of a Vespa. (*She resumes her seat*)

BEE. Vespa?

NAN. One of those little, low motor-bikes. It would be an invaluable time-saver when reconnoitring.

BEE (*rising*) I've never heard such madness.

NAN. Why?

BEE (*severely*) One of our most important rules is to behave like quiet and ordinary citizens. That does not include scorching about on motor-bicycles. (*She resumes her seat*)

NAN (*rising*) Mr Chairman, I insist on a vote being taken. (*She resumes her seat*)

BRIGADIER. Very well; we will vote by the usual show of hands. Those in favour?

(NAN *urgently holds up her hand*)

Those against?

(HATTIE, ALICE *and* BEE *hold up their hands*)

No motor-bicycle.

NAN (*rising, throwing down her book and moving down* L) I resign.

(HATTIE, ALICE *and* BEE *rise and cross to Nan, murmuring apologies*)

BRIGADIER (*ringing his bell*) Order, order, ladies.

ALICE (*coaxingly*) Bring it up at the next meeting.

NAN. Oh, all right.

(*They resume their seats*)

BRIGADIER. That brings us to the most important item— "Methods and Social Contacts". Lady Miller.

ALICE (*rising*) Mr Chairman—(*she gazes entranced at the Brigadier*)

(BEE *coughs*)

—Ladies. I simply must have new ideas for future operations. When we've used up (*with a loving glance at him*) Bertie's brilliant scheme on the great coup planned for tomorrow, the cupboard is bare.

BEE. You have my "dentist's waiting-room" idea.

ALICE. We can't do anything about that until we get the chloroform.

(*The* BRIGADIER *makes a note*)

The situation's very serious. So, please always be on the lookout. Examine the social, obituary and agony columns even more carefully; look about even more intently when meeting boat trains and aeroplanes; and bear in mind the urgent need for ideas wherever you go. (*She resumes her seat*)

(*The others applaud*)

BRIGADIER. I'm sure Alice won't mind if I add that you should be ready at all times to seize *unexpected* chances; what I might call "Targets of Fleeting Opportunity".

(*The others murmur "Fleeting Opportunity" uncomprehendingly*)

(*He rises*) Well, your reports represent a most commendable picture. If we complete tomorrow's important project satisfactorily . . .

BEE (*interrupting excitedly*) What about the plans? Have you got them ready?

BRIGADIER. To the last detail.

ALICE (*eagerly*) Oh, do let's hear them.

BRIGADIER. There are one or two more pieces of business upon the agenda.

BEE. Let them wait. The plans are much more exciting.

HATTIE. Oh, yes.

ALICE }
NAN } (*together*) Yes, yes.

BRIGADIER (*pleased*) Very well. If you insist. (*He picks up his clip-board, crosses to* L *and takes a knitting needle from the wool-basket below the desk*) They are rather neat.

(*The* BRIGADIER *releases a catch on the picture over the desk, and the picture swings open on a hinge, revealing a map of an area in South Kensington, covered with cellophane, on which there are markings in coloured pencil. For details see Plan "A"*)

BEE (*patting Hattie on the back; in a whisper*) A lovely piece of carpentry. Clever Hattie.

BRIGADIER (*ordering*) Gather round for briefing.

(ALICE, *rises, moves to the stool and sits on it.* NAN *rises, turns her chair to face* L *and resumes her seat.* BEE *rises, moves and stands above* Alice. HATTIE *rises, crosses and stands behind Bee*)

Pay close attention, please. (*He reads headings from his "orders"*) "Operation Ermine. *Information.* The enemy guard an ermine coat, value seven hundred and fifty pounds, in cold storage of fur department of store at 'X'. (*He points out the locations on the map with the knitting needle*) *Enemy Strength.* One: Mrs MacNaughton—head of fur department. Two: her half-witted assistant, name unknown. Three: Lily Thompson."

HATTIE. Oh, I don't think it's nice to call Lily "enemy".

BRIGADIER (*severely*) That is her category. Her effectiveness, however, is neutralized by the fact that tomorrow is her day off. During the period of the operation she will be at the cinematograph with her young man. (*He reads*) *Information own Troops.* That's us. Concentrated here, in flat, at "Y". *Intention.* Remove coat from "X" to "Y".

ALICE. Beautifully neat.

BEE. A model of compactness.

HATTIE. If only everything could be as clear as that.

BRIGADIER (*reading*) *Method.* An attack will be mounted tomorrow morning—at an "H" hour to be fixed. *Raiding party* will consist of *Appleby* and *Hatfield*. They will depart here at "H" minus six minutes, in Beatrice's death chariot.

(BEE *looks furious but dare not interrupt*)

Parry, up here, will create a diversion to deflect attention of hall porter from embussment.

HATTIE (*whispering*) "Embussment?"

BEE (*whispering*) Getting into the car.

BRIGADIER (*horribly patient*) Is something the matter, Miss Hatfield?

HATTIE (*scared*) No, no!

BRIGADIER (*thundering*) Then kindly pay attention. Raiding party will proceed—via Red Route—to parking place "P", at rear of store, arriving at "H" minus one.

BEE. Suppose there's a traffic block?

BRIGADIER (*furious at the interruption*) A margin of one minute has been allowed. Hatfield will *remain* in transport. Appleby will proceed on foot to store, arriving at main entrance at "H" hour exactly. To the other map, please. (*He crosses to the screen up* R)

(BEE *crosses and sits on the right end of the ottoman.* NAN *rises, crosses and sits on the left end of the ottoman, facing upstage.* ALICE *rises, crosses and stands by the fireplace.* HATTIE *remains* L, *staring at Plan "A"*)

(*He shouts*) Hatfield!

HATTIE *swings round nervously and sits on the chair* R *of the*

ACT II BREATH OF SPRING 33

table LC. *The* BRIGADIER *lets down a folding flap on the screen revealing an enlarged plan of the interior of store. For details see Plan "B"*)

Ground floor of store. Appleby will enter, and proceed—via Blue route—to the objective at "F", arriving there "H" plus two. At "H" plus one, Parry—(*pointing*) from that desk there—will engage Mrs MacNaughton in telephonic communication in curtained booth at rear of department. Appleby will render up forged cold-storage ticket to half-wit, taking coat in exchange. She will then proceed—via yellow route . . .

BEE. Yellow? It looks orange to me.

BRIGADIER (*shouting*) Yellow or orange, it's called "yellow". She will then proceed—via yellow route—to side entrance of store "S", and will embuss in waiting taxi. This will have been commandeered from rank "O" by Hatfield.

HATTIE. I feel dizzy when I think of it. You see, I . . .

BRIGADIER (*cutting in; loudly*) *Administration. Supplies.* These only consist of the eggs and oranges.

HATTIE (*rising*) Oh, yes, you've forgotten that part.

BRIGADIER (*horribly calmly*) I have not.

(HATTIE *resumes her seat*)

If Appleby has not reached taxi within two minutes of expected time . . .

HATTIE. I rush to the department——

BEE. —without appearing to hurry——

HATTIE. —and cause my "distraction".

ALICE (*nodding*) Firmly drop the shopping net on the floor.

HATTIE. Say the eggs don't break?

BRIGADIER (*annoyed*) They will! Anyhow, the oranges will roll about.

HATTIE. Then I faint?

BRIGADIER. *If* the situation demands it. *Medical and Veterinary.* Not applicable. *Dress.* Hatfield will camouflage herself as inconspicuously as possible. Appleby, on the other hand, will parade in outstanding piece of millinery.

BEE. I've prepared a lovely hat.

BRIGADIER. This important clue to identity will be destroyed immediately on completion of mission.

BEE. Shame.

BRIGADIER. *Intercommunication.* By hand-signal from window. *Questions.* Any?

BEE. None—it's wonderfully comprehensive.

ALICE. A gem.

BRIGADIER. Parry?

NAN (*rising and moving up* C) No questions, sir.

BRIGADIER. Hatfield?

HATTIE. Not for the moment, anyhow.

BRIGADIER. Good. Order Group, dismiss. (*He closes the map on the screen, then crosses and closes the picture*)
ALICE (*to Bee*) I do envy you having all that exciting part.
BEE. Well, you had all the fun during *Operation Kolinsky*.
BRIGADIER (*ringing his bell*) We'll close the board meeting, if you please.
BEE. Oh, there's nothing else important, is there?
NAN. We haven't discussed the question of overseas visitors, yet.
BEE. Oh, yes. We *must* amend the rules on that point. I don't think—(*she shakes her head distressfully*) it's fair to take from foreigners.
HATTIE. I think we should rule out wedding receptions, too.

(*There is a loud knock on the double doors*)

NAN. Lily!
BEE (*rising*) But it's silver-cleaning afternoon.
BRIGADIER. *Clearing action. Part A.* (*He hands his clip-board to Bee*)

(BEE *goes to the stool.* HATTIE *rises, collects the notebooks from the table and goes to the animal's head.* ALICE *collects the bell and goes to the cabinet down* R. NAN *collects the remaining papers, rolls them up and goes to the tusk above the fireplace*)

LILY (*off; calling*) I can't get in. What's happened?
BEE (*calling*) One moment, Lily.
BRIGADIER (*pointing to Bee*) Number one.

(BEE *puts the board in the concealed pocket under the stool seat. They all work slickly and very efficiently*)

(*He points to Hattie*) Number two.

(HATTIE *puts the notebooks inside the animal's head*)

(*He points to Alice*) Number three.

(ALICE *hides the bell in an ornament on the cabinet*)

(*He points to Nan*) Number four.

(NAN *puts the papers inside the tusk*)

Part B.

(HATTIE *rapidly replaces two upright chairs* R *and* L *of the double doors.* BEE *turns the desk chair to the desk.* NAN *and* ALICE *move to table to its Act I position.* BEE *places the other two upright chairs* R *and* L *of the table.* NAN *transfers the vase of flowers from the table behind the ottoman to the table up* L. *They then wait at attention*)

BEE (*reporting*) All correct.
BRIGADIER. Operation Relaxation.

ACT II   BREATH OF SPRING   35

(BEE *crosses and takes a book from the sideboard.* NAN *lolls on the ottoman, facing up stage.* ALICE *takes a magazine from the paper-rack and sits in the armchair down* R. HATTIE *gets a chessboard from the desk drawer, puts it on the table up* L, *then sits* L *of the table. The* BRIGADIER *gets four chessman from a jug on the cabinet up* LC, *puts them on the chessboard, then sits* R *of the table.* BEE *unlocks the door.*

LILY *enters from the hall, wearing her hat and coat and carrying her bag and gloves. She comes to* R *of Bee*)

(*He moves a chessman*) Check.
LILY. What on earth are you doing with the door locked?
BEE. We were ... (*She suddenly breaks off*) What on earth are *you* doing in your outdoor things?
LILY. That's what I came to tell you. I'm just off.
BEE. Just off? Just off where?
LILY. To the pictures with Bill.
BEE. To the pictures with Bill? (*With dawning horror*) But to-day's *Wednesday.* You go to the pictures with Bill *Thursdays.*
LILY. We had to change it to *today* this week, Dame dear.
HATTIE (*rising*) What!

(*The* BRIGADIER *glares at* HATTIE *who resumes her seat*)

BEE. But that means you'll be here tomorrow afternoon.
LILY (*nodding*) Doing the work I should be doing *this* afternoon. So it's just the same.
NAN (*rising and moving to Lily*) It's not all the same.
BRIGADIER (*rising*) You always go on Thursdays.
LILY. Now, don't you all start. I *have* to go today. Bill's mate's getting married tomorrow, so Bill's swopped turns with him.
BEE. No, no, he can't do that.
LILY. He has!
BEE. Well, he's to swop back again. And do the turn the station-master gave him. And take you out tomorrow afternoon, as usual.
LILY. Too late, Dame dear. Bill's mate's on the train by now. And Bill's in the foyer of the *Odeon* at Twickenham. I must fly. 'Bye.
BRIGADIER. No, wait.

(LILY *runs out, slamming the door behind her. A moment later the front door is heard to slam*)

NAN. Damnation.
HATTIE (*rising and moving to* L *of the Brigadier; agitatedly*) But we can't carry out "Operation Ermine" if she's here.
ALICE (*rising and moving below the ottoman*) What in heaven's name are we going to do?
BRIGADIER. Perhaps we can persuade her to go out with someone else tomorrow.

BEE. Not a hope—she's far too devoted to Bill.
HATTIE (*sitting* L *of the table*) Oh, what a disaster!
NAN. Could we lock her in her room tomorrow!
ALICE. What more suspicious?
NAN (*sitting on the ottoman and facing up stage*) True—oh, King!

(BEE, *after a moment's thought, moves down* C)

BEE. Why shouldn't we do the job this afternoon?
HATTIE (*rising*) No! No!
BRIGADIER (*thinking*) Everything's ready.
HATTIE (*agitatedly*) I'm not. I couldn't possibly carry out my part without going over it in my head the night before.
BEE. Of course you can.
BRIGADIER. We must make a snap decision. Immediate action or postponement?
NAN (*rising*) We *can't* postpone. The assistant who booked the coat is due back from hospital on Friday. She'd recognize Bee as not being the owner.
BEE. That settles it, then. It's this afternoon.
BRIGADIER. Very well—this afternoon. There's no time to be lost. *Prepare for Operation.* (*He looks at his watch*) *Assembly* here in—two minutes. I'll fetch my binoculars.

(*The* BRIGADIER *exits hurriedly to the hall*)

BEE. This dress will do. I'll get the special hat.

(BEE *exits quickly down* L. ALICE *crosses to the screen and opens the map.* NAN *puts the chessboard and chessmen on the desk, then opens the plan behind the picture*)

HATTIE. Oh, dear! I hate a rush. I'm sure something will go wrong. I only have the vaguest idea of what "H" minus anything means.
NAN. Rely on common sense.
HATTIE. I must rush and change my shoes in case I have to run.

(HATTIE *rushes out to the hall*)

ALICE. This would happen when it's our most important operation.
NAN. But it's a very quick one, and we've never had such a spanking scheme.
ALICE. Yes, it *must* be all right.
NAN. Touch wood! (*She touches the table*) Touch wood!

(BEE *hurries in down* L, *wearing an elaborately trimmed hat. She carries a piece of veiling, some hairpins, her handbag and her gloves. She crosses and sits on the left end of the ottoman*)

BEE (*to Alice; as she crosses*) Help me fix this wretched veil, will you?

ALICE. Ah! Beautifully conspicuous. Everyone will remember it. And no-one would dream *you'd* wear such a hat. (*She moves to Bee and assists her to fix the veil*)

NAN. Oh, the eggs and oranges. Luckily, I bought them this morning, but I haven't changed them into their shopping net yet.

(NAN *exits hurriedly to the hall*)

BEE (*nervously putting on her gloves*) One blessing about doing it in such a hurry—there isn't time for nerves.

ALICE. Darling, you needn't have the teeniest qualm. Bertie's plans always work quite marvellously.

BEE. His military knowledge has been an absolute boon, hasn't it?

ALICE. And how he's improved since he's had to use it again.

BEE. Yes, really back to his old form.

ALICE. So energetic, and managing, and charming . . .

BEE. A real delight to have about the house. (*She rises, crosses and looks at herself in the mirror on the mantelpiece*)

(ALICE *shoots a quick glance of suspicion at Bee*)

ALICE (*moving below the ottoman*) Darling, you haven't forgotten that I want him for a delight about *my* house?

BEE (*airily*) Oh, as I hadn't heard anything further, I imagined you'd given up the idea.

ALICE. You imagined wrong. It's just that I haven't had time to do anything about him.

BEE. Well, I shouldn't rush it, dear. This strength of character he's shown might be a little overwhelming. I wonder whether you'd be able to cope?

ALICE (*moving to* L *of Bee*) Are you quite sure you're not wondering whether you'd be able to cope?

(BEE *and* ALICE *look at each other.*
The BRIGADIER *enters hurriedly from the hall. He carries his pinger, and is hung about with the binoculars in case, a map case, the whistle, and a haversack*)

BRIGADIER (*moving to the fire-stool*) Everything ready? (*He takes the clip-board from the pocket under the stool*)

BEE (*crossing to* C) Is this all right?

BRIGADIER. A little more tipped over the eyes.

BEE. I've got to see to drive. (*Demonstrating*) I'll be quite unrecognizable with a handkerchief held up as if I had a cold.

(HATTIE *enters from the hall, putting on her hat and coat*)

HATTIE (*moving* R *of the table up* L; *mournfully*) Oh, dear, I feel awful. (*She puts her hand to her tummy*) Not just butterflies.

ALICE. Have a spoonful of your nerve tonic.

HATTIE. Just had one. It doesn't seem to act as it used to. I suppose because I'm an addict.

(NAN *enters hurriedly from the hall carrying a shopping net containing some oranges and eggs*)

NAN. The eggs and oranges. (*She hands them over to* HATTIE, *who holds them warily*)
BRIGADIER. Good. Now, any last moment points?
BEE. No, no, we could do it in our sleep.

(*The* BRIGADIER *puts the board and pinger on the table up* L, *and takes out his watch*)

BRIGADIER. Then very important; synchronize watches. (*He moves down* LC)

(*They move into a diagonal line.* HATTIE *is* R *of the Brigadier,* NAN *is* R *of Hattie.* BEE *is* R *of Nan and* ALICE R *of Bee. They all concentrate on their watches*)

ALICE (*worried*) Oh, dear—I never understand this part.
BRIGADIER (*ordering*) Fourteen thirty-six coming up—now.

(*There is a long pause while the others look bewildered.* BEE *counts on her fingers*)

HATTIE (*nervously*) Fourteen thirty-six—fourteen thirty-six? What exactly is that exactly?
BRIGADIER (*horribly patient*) Two thirty-six.
ALICE. Two thirty-six. I grovel with shame, but I can't even understand that.
BRIGADIER (*testily*) Twenty-four minutes to three.
ALICE. Amazing!
BEE. Twenty-four minutes to three? Oh, I think you're slow—I make it a quarter to three.
BRIGADIER (*explosively*) It doesn't matter whether I'm fast or slow. The only point is that we must all be the same.
NAN. But it must matter. If we're working on one time and the world on another . . .
BRIGADIER (*bellowing*) Of no account, of no account, of no account.
BEE (*crossing to* R *of the Brigadier; soothingly*) All right, all right. I'm changing mine to two thirty-six.
BRIGADIER (*very crossly*) Two thirty-eight now. Wait!

(*The others watch him*)

Now!

(*The others fiddle with their watches*)

Hurry along, hurry along. (*He crosses and stands behind the table up* L) We must commence operations. "H" hour is fourteen forty-

five. I'm setting the pinger. (*He sets the pinger. Ordering*) Engage the porter, Nan.
NAN. Which is on duty? The Boozer?
ALICE. Yes.
NAN. Good, he's easy. (*She crosses to the telephone, lifts the receiver and dials*)
BRIGADIER (*ordering*) Check equipment.
HATTIE (*moving to* R *of the table and holding up the shopping net*) Supplies.
BRIGADIER. Correct. Beatrice?

(HATTIE *moves* RC)

BEE (*moving to* R *of the table*) Ready.
BRIGADIER. Key of car?
BEE (*bringing the articles out of her handbag*) Yes.
BRIGADIER. List of timings?
BEE. Yes.
BRIGADIER. Clean handkerchief?
BEE (*nodding*) With ication marks removed.
BRIGADIER. Small change for taxi and gratuities?
BEE. Yes.
BRIGADIER. The forged cold-storage fur receipt?
BEE. Yes; and my smelling-salts. All correct. (*She replaces the articles in her bag*)
NAN (*into the telephone; with an extremely good American accent*) Hullo, is that the tall, wide and handsome porter? . . . Ah, now I want to speak with you, honey, so stay right there and hold the line. (*She covers the receiver and turns to the others*) All right.
BRIGADIER. Action! Good luck! (*He officially shakes hands with Bee and then with Hattie*)

(BEE *and* HATTIE *exit hurriedly by the front door.*

The BRIGADIER *gives Nan a signal to continue, then exits by the front door*)

NAN (*into the telephone*) Now, you see here, porter. Are you there? . . . Fine.

(ALICE *takes a cigarette from the box on the table behind the sofa, and lights it*)

Now, maybe this sounds kina crazy to you, but I want you to find me a little apartment in the gracious building of yours . . . Now, now, don't give me any of that sorry no soap stuff, because I'm just not going to listen . . . Yeah, yeah, yeah . . . But I'll see you're not sorry, dreamy fellow. (*She covers the telephone with her hand*)

(*The* BRIGADIER *enters by the front door, closes it and comes into the room.* NAN *looks anxiously at him*)

BRIGADIER. Just passing through hall. (*He moves to the balcony door. Urgently*) Don't let him escape. (*He goes on to the balcony*)
NAN (*into the telephone*) Maybe, like me you fancy a highball every little once in a while? . . . Well, my husband's in the liquor trade. If you accommodate us with the little home we're pining for, he'll let you have a bottle or two of Scotch periodically . . .

(*The* BRIGADIER *comes in from the balcony*)

BRIGADIER. All right; safely embussed.
NAN (*into the telephone*) A case or two? . . . (*Furiously*) Say, what do you think I am? Keep your damn flat. (*She replaces the receiver*)
ALICE (*sitting on the left end of the ottoman; admiringly*) I don't know how you do it.
NAN. My American students, dear. (*She sits on the fire-stool*)

(*There is a pause while they watch as the* BRIGADIER *moves to the desk, looks at his watch, takes a flag-marker from his haversack, and sticks it in the centre of "Red Route" on the plan. He then crosses to Plan "B"*)

ALICE. I do hope Hattie's nerves won't make her do anything silly.
NAN. Yes, the poor beast gets so het-up. But she'd be jolly hurt if we left her out.
BRIGADIER. She's all right behind the flutter; I've had experience of her sort.
NAN (*rising and moving to the double doors*) While we're waiting for the "pinger" I'll put the kettle on. They'll be in need of a cup when they get back.
BRIGADIER. Don't be long: your next call is the vital one.
NAN. Shan't be a jiffy.

(NAN *exits to the hall, closing the doors behind her*)

ALICE (*rising and crossing to the window*) I hate this waiting period. I'd much rather be taking an active part, however alarming.

(*The* BRIGADIER *sits on the left end of the ottoman. During the following speeches he concentrates on his watch and "orders", much to* ALICE'S *annoyance*)

BRIGADIER. My dear Alice, it's well known that it's far less worrying to be a private in the front line, than the general safely in operational H.Q.
ALICE. Oh, is it? (*She wanders down* L, *and then to the cabinet up* LC)
BRIGADIER. Now, sit down, and relax; you're looking quite flushed.
ALICE. Fancy you noticing. (*She moves to* L *of the Brigadier.*

Cooingly) I thought I could go about in a yashmak without it catching your eye.

BRIGADIER (*huffily*) I've always been particularly observant.

ALICE (*hastily*) Of course you have; it was a silly joke to try and take our minds off the operation.

(*The* BRIGADIER *grunts.* ALICE *moves above the table up* L)

BRIGADIER (*impatiently*) Do sit down, my dear!

ALICE. Yes, it's absurd to worry. (*With a glance at him*) And a waste of time. (*She goes to the fire-stool, moves it to* L *of the Brigadier and sits on it*) What we should have done without you I tremble to think.

BRIGADIER. I dare say you'd have managed.

ALICE. We shouldn't. We should have been sheep without a shepherd. (*With a sad little glance at him*) That's how I often feel nowadays; a wandering sheep without a shepherd. Can you understand that, Bertie?

BRIGADIER. I never allow myself to mope.

ALICE (*overcoming the setback, and trying again*) Of course, you wouldn't. But I'm tired of being at the beck and call of waiters and chambermaids. I want my own home again. With my own bits and pieces around me. (*Casually*) Are yours still in warehouse?

BRIGADIER (*nodding*) Costing a fortune.

ALICE (*brightly*) Why not let me help you sort out the better pieces one day?

BRIGADIER (*falling into the trap*) What would I do with them?

ALICE. Perhaps we could find you a little flat to put them in.

BRIGADIER. I never want the bother of a flat again.

ALICE (*coercingly*) You'd be all right with someone to help you run it?

BRIGADIER. Do you think so? (*He looks up and puts his clip-board on the seat of the ottoman beside him*) I'd never have considered it six months ago. But I'm wondering now if there's *anything* we couldn't do.

ALICE. Of course there isn't! A beautiful thought, Bertie. We still have wonderful years ahead of us.

BRIGADIER (*moving closer to her*) Enthusiasm was always one of your most becoming traits, Alice. By jove, I've a good mind to . . .

(*The pinger goes off with a loud ping*)

"H" hour! (*He jumps up, moves to the double doors and opens them*)

ALICE. Damn!

BRIGADIER (*speaking off; in a loud whisper*) Nan! The attack's started. Where the devil is the woman? (*He turns*) Dial the shop, Alice, or we'll be late. The number's in red on my board. (*He turns and calls louder*) Nan!

(ALICE *rises, refers to the clip-board, then crosses to the telephone, lifts the receiver and dials*)

ALICE. I won't speak. I couldn't decive an imbecile.

(*The* BRIGADIER *crosses to the map down* L, *removes the flag, closes the map, takes the clip-board from Alice, then crosses to Plan "B".*
NAN *enters hurriedly from the hall*)

BRIGADIER. Nan! It's time.

NAN (*rushing to Alice and taking the receiver from her*) Sorry—cutting bread and butter. (*Into the telephone. With a strong and excellent French accent*) 'Ullo? 'Ullo? ... Je veux parler avec Madame MacNaughton, s'il vous plaît? ... I wish to converse with Madame MacNaughton, please ... Moi? ... I am Mademoiselle—(*she thinks frantically*) Du Bonnet. Of the Parisian Publicity Circle ... You are too kind ... (*To the others*) Fetching her. I knew the word "publicity" would work the trick.

BRIGADIER (*closely studying his watch, "orders" and plan*) If she comes to the telephone straight away we'll be all right. Beatrice has entered the shop, and is passing through—(*he sticks a marker flag in the plan*) "haberdashery". (*He turns to Nan*) Nothing?

NAN. Not yet.

(*They wait*)

BRIGADIER (*moving the flag*) She's through haberdashery and entering "blouses".

ALICE. We should have thought of a surer method of getting Mrs MacNaughton out of the way.

NAN. We've used the fire scare too often.

(*They wait again, becoming alarmed*)

BRIGADIER. No sound?
NAN. No.
BRIGADIER (*horrified*) She's through "blouses", and entering "gowns". Another fifteen seconds and she'll be at "furs".
ALICE. This is ghastly. Do you think ... ?
NAN. Shh! (*Into the telephone*) 'Ullo? ... Madame MacNaughton? ... Bon ...
BRIGADIER. Thank Heavens.

(NAN *stuffs her handkerchief into the the mouthpiece*)

NAN. I am so sorry—you are very 'ard to 'ear ... Can you 'ear me? Sacre nom de chien! Hold a moment; I will give it a little knock. (*She bangs the receiver on the desk*) Is that better? ... Bon ...

BRIGADIER. Don't spin it out too long, or she may become suspicious.

NAN. Madame MacNaughton, I represent the Paris Publicity

ACT II BREATH OF SPRING

Circle. We are running a series of articles "Les Femmes du Grande Monde". "Women who have Reached the Top." Will you honour me by featuring in it? . . .

ALICE (*whispering*) With photographs; she's as vain as a peacock.

NAN. With photographs, of course . . . (*Cooing*) Mais oui; Bien sur, you will easily outshine the others. You are so chic, so charmante, so elegante—so ravissante . . .

BRIGADIER (*moving c and keeping his eye on his watch and "orders"*) "H" plus four minutes.

NAN. Bon . . . I will write and confirm . . . (*She cocks an eye at the Brigadier as she speaks*) Now, let me see—is there anything else? . . .

BRIGADIER. Should be well clear of the store by now. (*He nods to Nan*) Safe.

NAN. No, that is everything . . . Not at all. Thank you. (*She replaces the receiver and sits, mopping her brow*)

ALICE (*clapping*) Bravo! Bravo!

(*The* BRIGADIER *removes the flag from Plan "B" and closes it*)

BRIGADIER. If Hattie had the cab waiting, they'll have started on their way back. (*Ordering*) Prepare for next stage—"Distraction of porter during Re-entry". (*He takes a small box from his haversack, extracts a diamond ring and hands it to Alice*) Here's the ring.

ALICE. But this is too good, Bertie. Suppose it really gets lost?

BRIGADIER. Beatrice paid sixpence at Woolworth's between the wars.

ALICE. Halcyon days! (*She crosses, goes out on the balcony, looks down, then re-enters the room*) He's just outside the front entrance. Shall I start?

BRIGADIER. Another fifteen seconds. Better take up your position, Nan, in case they're running early.

(NAN *rises, gets the binoculars from the case round his neck, stands on the beer crate* L *of the window and "observes"*)

(*He concentrates on his watch*) Five, four, three, two, one. Action, Alice!

(ALICE *throws the ring out of the window, in the opposite direction to the balcony, into the street below, then goes on to the balcony*)

ALICE (*calling*) Porter! Porter! (*Running back into the room*) Damn! The other one's on duty now—the deaf one. (*She runs out on to the balcony, waves and calls*) Porter! Porter!

NAN. From the diaphragm, Alice—forward on the lips. (*She demonstrates and calls loudly*) Porter! Porter!

ALICE (*calling*) Porter! Porter! (*She chokes and comes into the room, coughing violently*)

(*The* BRIGADIER *pats Alice on the back*)

If we use this way again, it will pay us to give him a hearing-aid. (*She runs on to the balcony and calls*) Porter! Up here! Me! Lady Miller. Something awful has happened, Porter. Dame Beatrice was playing with a diamond ring on her finger, and it slipped off. Just by the letter-box. (*She listens*) Yes, please do. (*She runs back into the room. To Nan*) Any sign of them yet?
    NAN (*watching*) No.
    BRIGADIER. There should be. I trust nothing's gone wrong.
    ALICE (*calling through the window in the direction to where the Porter has now moved*) Do hurry, Porter.
    BRIGADIER (*getting panicky*) They should have been in sight at "H" plus seven. It's "H" plus eight.
    ALICE. I can't play him forever.
    NAN (*scanning*) There must have been a hitch of some sort.
    ALICE. They can't have been caught?
    BRIGADIER. If they're not in sight immediately, we'll have to assume the worst.
    NAN (*appalled*) Put Plan "Z" into operation?
    ALICE (*horrified*) Oh, surely not!
    BRIGADIER. Well, at least part one of "Z".
    ALICE. Oh, this is ghastly! (*Looking out of the window*) No sign, Porter? (*To the Brigadier*) What can I do?

    (NAN *gets off the box and moves to the upstage end of the windows*)

(*Agitatedly*) He'll see it any minute!
    BRIGADIER. Confuse him somehow.
    ALICE. Confuse him? (*She thinks desperately, sees her bag, throws it out of the downstage end of the window, then goes back to where she threw the ring and calls*) Porter! Now I've dropped my bag.
    NAN. Shall I whizz round to the shop in a cab?
    BRIGADIER. It might only result in another in the net. (*Horrified*) "H" plus ten. (*Bravely*) It's plan "Z".
    ALICE. Oh, *no!* It's too drastic.
    NAN. They'd agree if they were here. (*She turns and looks through the binoculars*)
    BRIGADIER. Yes. We mustn't allow sentiment to stand in the way of duty. Alice, dial nine-nine-nine. I'll get my revolver. (*He moves towards the double doors*)
    NAN (*excitedly*) Wait! I think I see the cab, now. Yes! Yes, there's the flutter of the handkerchief from the window. (*She dances*) Tolderolloli!
    ALICE. Heaven be praised!
    BRIGADIER. Porter well out of the way, Alice?
    ALICE (*calling out of the window*) More to the right—to the right. (*She turns into the room*) All clear.
    BRIGADIER. Action, Nan.

    (NAN *waves a handkerchief three times across her window*)

NAN (*commentating*) The cab's drawing up now . . . They must have paid from the back of the cab because they've gone straight in . . . They've disappeared . . . Cab driving off.
BRIGADIER (*to Nan*) Did they look alarmed?
NAN (*turning into the room*) Couldn't see—(*she puts the binoculars on the table up* L) they hurried in with their heads down.
BRIGADIER (*putting his board on the table up* L) I'll do the front door—they won't be a moment if the lift's free. (*He goes into the hall and stands by the front door*)
ALICE (*calling out of the window*) Oh, what a blessing! Could you bring them up? You're a dear, clever man. (*She shouts*) I said: "Dear, clever man."
NAN. Remind me to give you some breathing exercises.

(ALICE *moves down* L. *There are three loud knocks on the front door. The* BRIGADIER *opens it.*
BEE *sails in quickly. She wears a full-length ermine coat.*
HATTIE, *very woebegone, follows* BEE *in. She carries her shopping net. The* BRIGADIER *closes the front door.* BEE *comes into the room and pirouettes gaily, floating the coat out round her, and ends in a curtsy.* HATTIE *comes into the room, puts the shopping net on the table up* L, *then stands up* C)

BEE (*moving to* R *of Alice*) Et le voila, mesdames, messieurs!

(*The* BRIGADIER *comes into the room, closes the double doors, and stands up* R *of Bee*)

ALICE. Darling! I've never been so relieved to see anyone.

(NAN *crosses and sits on the stool,* R *of Bee*)

NAN. What on earth happened?
BEE. We had a little hold-up. We'll talk about it later.
ALICE. We'll talk about it now. You can't frighten us out of our lives, and then not explain.
BEE. Yes, I can.
HATTIE (*moving round* R *of the ottoman*) Oh, they may as well hear now. (*She moves below the ottoman and sits on it*) It was me. I was—sick.
ALICE. Hattie, you poor thing.
BEE (*putting her handbag on the table up* L) Fortunately, I had a carrier-bag in the back of the car.
HATTIE. I must have swallowed nerve tonic too quickly after treacle pudding.
BRIGADIER. Did all go well, other than this—unpleasantness?
BEE. To the second. It was almost too easy, wasn't it, Hattie?
HATTIE. I wouldn't say that.
BEE. The half-wit handed it over without so much as a glance of suspicion.
ALICE. Let me have a proper look, Bee.

D

BRIGADIER (*crossing to the stove*) Before relaxing, let us complete the mission, if you please.

BEE. Yes, you're right, Bertie. (*She removes her hat. Sadly*) We must burn the chief evidence. (*To Nan*) You do it. I should feel I was committing infanticide.

(NAN *crosses and takes the hat from Bee, then crosses to the stove*)

ALICE. Think of the delicious replacement you can buy out of expenses.

(*The* BRIGADIER *opens the stove and* NAN *puts the hat in. The front door bell rings.* BEE *rises, slips out of the coat and hands it to Alice*)

BRIGADIER (*closing the stove*) That's the porter with the ring, and Alice's handbag.

HATTIE (*rising and moving up* C) I'll go.

BRIGADIER. No, no. He must see Beatrice. In case of a wanted alibi.

BEE (*moving to the double doors*) I'll ask him about the weather as if I hadn't been out all day. (*She looks towards the stove and sniffs*) Rest in peace, dear friend.

(BEE *exits to the hall, closing the doors behind her*)

HATTIE (*crossing to* R *of Alice and stroking the coat*) I've never seen such an exquisite ermine.

ALICE. Easily our best so far.

BRIGADIER (*crossing to* R *of Hattie*) Even better than I expected from the glimpse of the reconnoitre.

NAN (*crossing to* R *of the Brigadier*) So smooth and silky—(*she pats the coat*) like a well-conditioned animal.

BRIGADIER. That really will increase our funds.

ALICE. Yes; we shall have a small fortune to distribute. Lovely!

HATTIE (*taking the coat*) It's so light! I must just . . . (*She slips the coat on*)

BRIGADIER. Now, no dilly-dallying, Hattie dear.

HATTIE. Only for a moment, Brigadier. (*She crosses with a mannequin's walk and stands down* R) I suddenly understand why women become wicked.

BRIGADIER (*moving up* R *of the ottoman*) Hattie, rule thirteen—"immediate concealment".

(HATTIE *removes the coat and puts it on the ottoman.*
BEE *enters hastily from the hall and quickly closes the door behind her. She carries Alice's handbag*)

BEE (*in a loud whisper*) Look out! Danger! (*She locks the door*)

(*They all lower their voices*)

BRIGADIER. What?

BEE (*moving* C) Lily's back.
BRIGADIER ⎱ (*together*) ⎰ Lily!
ALICE ⎰   ⎱ Impossible!
NAN (*rising and moving below the ottoman*) She can't have got back from Twickenham.
BEE. When I turned from the front door, there she was down the passage, looking at me.
ALICE. Did she say anything?
BEE. No.
HATTIE. What did you say?
BEE. I was so surprised to see her I just blurted out—"Bring tea".
NAN. She won't be long, then—I'd put the kettle on.
BRIGADIER (*ordering*) Emergency Clearing Action! Key, Nan. (*He crosses, picks up his clip-board and moves down* L)

(NAN *gets a key from the handle of the parasol hanging on the wall down* R, *and unlocks the ottoman.* HATTIE *collects her shopping-net and drops some oranges*)

(*He puts down the board in the wool-basket down* L, *turns and sees oranges*) Don't cause your distraction now. (*He kicks the oranges*)

(HATTIE *runs about collecting the oranges.* ALICE *takes the net and oranges from Hattie and puts them in the ottoman.* NAN *puts the coat in the ottoman, locks it and conceals the key in the parasol. The* BRIGADIER, *assisted by* ALICE, *hides the pinger and binoculars and haversack, map case and whistle in the plinth*)

BEE (*moving to the double doors*) Is it safe to relax?
BRIGADIER (*after looking round the room*) All clear.

(NAN *takes four newspapers from the paper-rack and gives one each to Hattie, Alice and Bee.* HATTIE *crosses and sits down* R. NAN *stands by the fireplace.* ALICE *sits on the ottoman. The* BRIGADIER *picks up a copy of "The Times" from the desk and sits in the desk chair.* BEE *unlocks the door then sits on the stool* C)

We'll tie up all loose ends after refreshment.
BEE. Yes, I'll change into something different after tea to fetch the car.
BRIGADIER. It's very tiring for you. I wish one of us could drive.
NAN. I drive perfectly well; I just can't pass the damn test.
ALICE. Try bribery next time.

(*There is a tap on the double doors which then opens*)

BEE (*she motions the others to read their papers*) Ah, this'll be Lily with our tea.

(LILY *enters by the double doors. She has removed her coat and has a determined expression*)

LILY (*moving* C) No, it won't. We're not having tea.
BEE. What!
LILY (*firmly*) We're having an understanding instead.
BEE. Listen, Lily . . .
LILY (*interrupting*) No, you listen to me, Dame dear. I'm not going to have you all ending up behind bars.
BRIGADIER (*rising and trying to bluster it out*) What the devil are you talking about?
LILY. You know very well what I'm talking about, you naughty old Brigadier.
BRIGADIER. Miss Thompson!
LILY. I've had my suspicions of you all for some time. So this afternoon I thought I'd pretend to go out, and see what happened. (*With a gesture*) Though Gawd knows, I never expected nothing like this.
BEE (*rising*) You've been watching us this afternoon?
LILY. I have.
NAN (*rising*) Christmas!

(HATTIE *and* ALICE *rise*)

LILY. I need my head examining, but I'm too fond of you all to let you be caught.

(BEE *sits on the stool*)

Which is what you're going to be as sure as my name's Lily Thompson.
ALICE. But we're wonderfully successful.
LILY. How, beats me. My blood ran cold when I saw the risks you took. And for what?
HATTIE (*proudly*) A very valuable ermine coat.
LILY. Ermine, my foot! Squirrel.
NAN (*horrified*) Squirrel?

(HATTIE *sits in the chair down* R)

LILY. Squirrel. Let's have a look.
BRIGADIER. Key, Nan.

(NAN *gets the key, unlocks the ottoman and opens it.* BEE *rises, takes out the coat and gives it to Lily*)

BEE (*crossing down* L) You're wrong, Lily. We heard the owner say it was ermine. And the shop accepted it as ermine.
LILY. Fancy believing what shops say. (*She examines the coat*) Worked to *imitate* ermine, but dyed Canadian squirrel.
ALICE (*furiously*) How dare people be so dishonest!
HATTIE. Dyed Canadian squirrel?
NAN (*sitting on the edge of the ottoman*) I'd have sworn it was ermine.

ACT II BREATH OF SPRING

LILY. Even if it was—what's the use of fiddling about with ermine? The only fur that brings in real lolly is mink.
BEE. Oh?
LILY. Not any old mink, either. Just the mutation minks—Sapphire, Royal Pastel and Silver Blue.
ALICE. Really?
LILY. You see, you haven't a clue! You can't hope to get away with so little knowledge.
ALICE. We're learning all the time.
LILY (*putting the coat on the stool and moving down to Nan; strongly*) Look! I've known blokes who've watched all the basic points: fingerprints, dogs, sufficient preparation, (*moving to Hattie*) type of window-catches, floor coverings, keys, locks, telephones and burglar alarms. (*Moving back to Brigadier*) Blokes who've spent weeks studying the three "H's" . . .
BRIGADIER. The three "H's"?
LILY. Habits, Hobbies and Holidays. They've known their victim's favourite wireless and telly programmes, who baths when, who's courting who, and who sleeps where. Even *they've* been caught! How can *you* hope to escape?
BRIGADIER (*shamefacedly*) Points we haven't paid much attention to.
LILY (*very seriously*) You've been *horribly* lucky so far. But it can't last.
BEE (*sitting in the desk chair*) You're exaggerating the danger, Lily.
LILY (*almost shouting*) I'm not! Take my advice, or else there's going to be great blaring headlines soon: (*tracing the words with her hands*) "Albert Memorial Fur Gang Grabbed".
HATTIE (*terrified*) Lily, don't!
LILY. "Police Pounce on Guilty Group."
BEE (*trying to brave it out*) Stop it, Lily.
LILY (*turning to Bee*) No; it's *you* who've got to stop it. Otherwise, Dame dear, there's going to be a ring at the front door one day, and it'll be the police. (*She goes down* C *and faces them*) With a great big Black Maria. I'll make you a strong pot of tea to wash the thought down with.

The front-door bell rings loudly. Everyone freezes. LILY *moves two steps up* C. *The bell rings again.* LILY *moves to the double doors. As she does so, the others quickly hide.*

BEE *rises and exits down* L. ALICE *goes behind the screen up* R. *The* BRIGADIER *hides behind the window curtains.* HATTIE *rises, crosses and crawls under the table up* L. NAN *rises, gets into the ottoman and closes the lid.* LILY *stops and turns to find everyone gone, then* NAN's *hand appears from the ottoman and pulls the fur into it.* LILY *stares at the disappearing fur as—*

the CURTAIN *quickly falls*

ACT III

SCENE—*The same. Six months later. Afternoon.*
There is a further alteration in the positions of the furniture. The table behind the ottoman is now down L with the desk chair behind it. The tub chairs is LC with the stool R of it. There is an upright chair in front of the cabinet up LC and another above the door down L. The vases and bowls are now full of spring flowers. The screen is folded.

When the CURTAIN *rises, it is about four o'clock. There is a pile of good furs draped over the tub chair and stool, each with a label or ticket. The ottoman is open. The* BRIGADIER *is seated in the desk chair at the table down* L, *checking a list. His clip-board and pinger are on the table along with a few small labels or tickets and some pins.* BEE *is standing* C, *holding a luxurious mink coat and looking business-like wi h a pair of scissors on a ribbon and a tape-measure round her neck.* ALICE *is sitting on the edge of the open ottoman, handing out furs. They are stock-taking.* BEE *finishes examining the coat, and passes it in silence to the* BRIGADIER *who adds a small numbered ticket to it.*

BEE (*moving behind the pile of furs and rubbing her hands*) Oh, I do love stocktaking.
BRIGADIER (*throwing the coat on to the pile*) Next?
ALICE (*taking a fur from the ottoman*) The coat from the Harley Street psychiatrist's wife. (*She passes the coat to Bee*)
BEE (*spreading the coat out in front of her*) Canadian ranch mink, cocktail sleeves and double fur collar. Five hundred pounds.
BRIGADIER (*writing on his list*) "Five hundred."
BEE (*moving to R of the Brigadier*) Though the skins are a bit hard on the leather. We'd better be prepared to accept four hundred.
BRIGADIER (*making the correction*) "Four hundred."
BEE. It'll probably have the cutter's initials in indelible pencil on a tape inside here. (*She opens the lining at the bottom of the coat with a few deft snips with her scissors*)
ALICE (*admiringly*) Darling, you are clever.
BEE. It's our new ex-army fence who's clever. I merely put into practice what he teaches me. (*She shows the coat*) Yes; the late owner's name, too! Just as well I looked. (*She hands the coat to the Brigadier, then crosses above the tub chair to* L *of the ottoman*) They'll have to be cut out, and the lining restitched.
BRIGADIER. I'll add it to the "Pre-Disposal Alteration List". (*He makes a note, pins a ticket to the coat and throws it on to the pile*) Next?
ALICE (*taking the mink coat from the ottoman*) The film actress's cloak. (*She passes the fur to Bee*)

BEE. Jasmine mink with fox cuffs. Very special. We should get a thousand.
ALICE. No!
BEE (*crossing and handing the fur to the Brigadier*) To think when I was a girl, mink was only used for lining carriage rugs. (*She crosses to* L *of the ottoman*)
BRIGADIER (*adding a ticket to the coat and looking at his watch*) Where the devil are Nan and Hattie? (*He throws the coat on the pile*) They knew stocktaking was at fifteen forty-five. (*He notes the coat on his list*)
ALICE. It couldn't mean they've been caught?
BEE. No, no. Nan's always late on her day off. And Hattie's so worried about being followed that she wastes hours changing buses.
BRIGADIER. Her nerves have been worse than ever since we had that Black Maria scare.
ALICE. So have mine, for that matter. I can't think of it without hearing handcuffs rattling.
BEE (*angrily*) That newspaper boy hasn't forgotten the rattling I gave him for ringing like that.
BRIGADIER. Next?
ALICE (*passing another fur to Bee*) The Hanover Street job.
BEE (*examining the fur*) Finest quality chinchilla.
ALICE. One of our most difficult operations.
BEE. Yes, indeed.
ALICE. This is heaven! Our profits will be ten times more than in the first six months.
BRIGADIER. That's a conservative estimate.
BEE (*crossing to* R *of the Brigadier*) Splendid! We shall be able to help people outside the London area soon. (*She hands the fur to the Brigadier*) A very rare fur nowadays; but rather noticeable; two hundred pounds. (*She crosses above the ottoman*)

(*The* BRIGADIER *makes a note and tosses the fur on to the pile*)
No alterations.

(*The double doors are flung open.*
HATTIE *enters breathless from the hall. She carries a rather poor, short mole fur coat over her arm, covered by her plastic raincoat*)

HATTIE (*moving* C; *excitedly*) What do you think?
ALICE. You've been followed again.
HATTIE. No, no. (*She moves to* R *of the Brigadier. Proudly*) I've taken advantage of one of your "Targets of Fleeting Opportunity" Brigadier.
BRIGADIER. No!
HATTIE. Yes. I've never quite understood what you meant, but when I saw one this morning I recognized it in a flash. (*She crosses to* C) And here it is. (*She proudly holds up the mole fur coat*)

BEE (*glumly*) Oh, yes. Mole. (*She leans against the lid of the ottoman*)
HATTIE (*hurt*) Oh, I know it's not mink. But considering I carried out the whole task myself, I rather expected congratulations.
ALICE. My dear, your courage robbed us of words.
BRIGADIER (*unconvincingly*) Yes, you've done well. How did you get it?
HATTIE (*enthusiastically*) It was during my "Look-and-Listen" tour of duty. I worked the Park Lane area. I did two of those coffee-bar places without hearing or seeing anything hopeful. So I thought I'd change to tea, force down a cup, and then call it a day. I went to the *Pink Parakeet*—you know the one?
ALICE. Indeed! Candlelight and stale cakes.
HATTIE. I sat down at an empty table, and there on a chair beside me was this coat—and no sign of the owner. (*She moves above the tub chair*) So I just slipped it on, and walked out.
BEE. Hattie, how brave!
HATTIE. I got on the first bus I saw, and it took me to Herne Hill. I spent a lovely afternoon there, letting the scent get cold.
BRIGADIER (*not very happily*) We must discuss these fleeting opportunities at the next meeting. I'll add it to the list.

(HATTIE *passes the coat to the* BRIGADIER *who makes a note, labels it and puts it on the pile*)

HATTIE. Have I missed stocktaking?
BEE. We've almost finished.
BRIGADIER. But you've come at the right moment. Lily may be back early; watch, will you?
HATTIE (*taking up a position at the window*) Clear immediately I give the signal, won't you? My heart misses a beat when I think of her finding us still carrying on.
BEE. We're quite safe with all our extra precautions.
BRIGADIER (*to Alice*) Come along. Come along. Next.
ALICE (*taking a fur cape from the ottoman*) The last. This charming mink we got at the opera. (*She passes the cape to Bee*)
BEE (*putting the cape round her shoulders*) Wild mink shrug cape with yoke collar.
HATTIE (*crossing to* L *of Bee*) Oh, how gorgeous. (*She strokes the fur*)
BRIGADIER (*fiercely*) Stay at your post, Hattie!
HATTIE (*skipping back to the window*) Sorry!
BEE (*crossing to* R *of the Brigadier*) Three hundred pounds. (*Blowing on the fur*) Oh, there are tufts of white hair on the outside edge.
ALICE. I expect the owner had them left purposely: they're supposed to be lucky.

BRIGADIER. When she finds she's lost the fur, she'll realize the fallacy of that superstition.
ALICE (*laughing fondly*) Bertie, you really are most witty. And getting more so every day.
BEE (*with a glance at Alice*) I thought it a remark in rather doubtful taste. Anyhow, they're easily traced. (*She hands the fur to the Brigadier, moves to the table up* L *and discards her scissors and tape-measure*) They must be plucked out.
BRIGADIER (*making a note*) Noted. (*He labels the fur and tosses it on the pile*)

(NAN *enters hurriedly from the hall, closing the doors behind her. She wears outdoor clothes and carries a basket which she puts down near the ottoman*)

NAN. Sorry to be so late.
BEE. Have you had a good day, dear?
NAN. Anything but. My sister's got boils . . .
ALICE. Oh, the poor thing.
NAN. But far worse; my fur coat has been stolen!

(*The others exclaim in horror*)

Aunt Letty only passed it on to me last week.
HATTIE. Nan, how dreadful!
BRIGADIER. Where did you lose it?
NAN. In the *Pink Parakeet*.
HATTIE. Oh! (*In complete silence she crosses guiltily to the pile of furs and picks up the mole*) Is this it?
NAN (*taking the coat*) My mole! Whatever is it doing there?
HATTIE (*faintly*) I took it from the *Pink Parakeet*.
NAN. Hattie!
HATTIE (*almost in tears*) Oh, I am sorry. I was so proud, too. Oh, dear, oh, dear!
NAN (*patting Hattie strongly on the back*) There, there, old girl. It's such a relief to have it back that I'm almost glad you took it.
BEE. It's the sort of mistake any of us might make.
HATTIE (*wailing*) I thought I'd been so clever.
NAN. You were! I was only away two minutes.
HATTIE (*cheering up*) Hadn't anyone any idea how it had gone?
NAN. Not the foggiest. I sent for the dunderhead of a manager, said he must report it, and threatened to sue them. But the poor beast hadn't a clue. You were jolly cunning.
HATTIE. Oh, thank you, Nan. From you who carried out the Brompton Road job so brilliantly, that *is* praise.

(NAN *puts the mole on the chair* L *of the double doors*)

BRIGADIER. You all deserve praise. (*He indicates the pile of furs*) This is a splendid batch.
ALICE (*rising and moving down* R; *urgently*) But we must get them

off to the fence. If they were found here it would be disastrous.
HATTIE (*nervously*) Don't even think of it! (*She returns to her post at the window*)
BEE. The garage says the car will be mended tomorrow. We'll take them when it gets dark.
HATTIE (*suddenly*) Cave! Lily crossing the road.
BRIGADIER (*rising*) Concealing Drill. Commence!

(ALICE *kneels in front of the ottoman.* NAN, BEE *and the* BRIGADIER *form a line* L *of the ottoman and pass furs rapidly and systematically along the line to* ALICE *who puts them in the ottoman. The* BRIGADIER *then hides all papers and his board in the wool-basket down* L. NAN *locks the ottoman*)

NAN. Locked.
BRIGADIER. Hattie. (*He points to her*)

(HATTIE *lowers the upstage hanging basket.* NAN *crosses and puts the key in the basket and* HATTIE *raises it again*)

BEE. We'd better disperse.
ALICE (*rising and crossing to the double doors*) Yes, good idea. Come back to my hotel, Bertie, and I'll give you a delicious cup of tea.
BRIGADIER. That's very kind of you, my dear. (*He moves towards Alice*)
BEE (*quickly intercepting the Brigadier; after a moment's rapid thought*) I'm sorry, but there's something I *must* discuss with you, Bertie. I'm sure you'll forgive me, Alice?

(ALICE's *expression is anything but forgiving*)

HATTIE (*moving to Alice and taking her arm*) Come and have a cup of tea in my room, Alice.

(NAN *exits to the hall*)

ALICE. Well, I don't really ...
HATTIE. I've a rather nice Swiss roll.
ALICE. I never eat with my tea.

(NAN *enters from the hall*)

NAN. Hurry! We'll get copped.
ALICE. I often wonder why I'm your friend, Bee.

(HATTIE *and* NAN *bustle the lingering* ALICE *into the hall, follow her off and close the doors behind them. The* BRIGADIER *moves to* L *of the ottoman*)

BEE (*moving* C) It's nice to have a moment to ourselves, isn't it? The one drawback of our organization is that it gives so little time for private matters. Sit down, Bertie.

Act III   BREATH OF SPRING   55

BRIGADIER (*sitting on the left end of the ottoman*) I enjoy being kept busy.

BEE (*moving the stool to* L *of the ottoman*) Oh, so do I. But we must be careful not to become like the Americans, and have business success at the cost of personal happiness.

BRIGADIER. I see what you're getting at.

BEE (*wondering if he does*) Good. (*She sits on the stool*) Because what I want to discuss with you, Bertie, is the question of holidays.

BRIGADIER. Holidays?

BEE. As far as business is concerned, the coming summer months will be a "close season".

BRIGADIER. "Close season", of course! But there's always "planning" and "preparation".

BEE. Yes, but a holiday would freshen us all up. (*Coaxingly*) Wouldn't you enjoy a nice lazy rest in the sun?

BRIGADIER (*glumly*) It poured every hour of the ten days I had at Bournemouth last year.

BEE (*trying again*) Ah, but I was thinking of somewhere where one can be sure of sun—such as the Riviera. Think how lovely Monte Carlo used to be in the late spring.

BRIGADIER (*shuddering*) I've known it so cold that I've had to wear an overcoat and muffler.

BEE (*annoyed*) Quite exceptional. (*Charming him again*) Usually it's heavenly. Think what a delightful change to sit under the mimosa trees, and talk of old times.

BRIGADIER. Mimosa gives me hay-fever.

BEE (*furious*) Under the palm trees, then. (*She controls herself*) What fun we had. (*She chuckles*) Do you remember the dinner-party when Madame Constantine said she'd pay for as much champagne as we could drink?

BRIGADIER (*chuckling*) I remember how shocked she was when we all joined in with the orchestra, using our asparagus-tongs as castanets.

BEE. I'd forgotten that. (*She laughs*) Afterwards I solemnly bowed to a strangely-dressed woman in the lift, and then saw it was my own reflection in the mirror with my evening cape on inside out.

(*They rock with laughter*)

BRIGADIER. Yes, yes, we certainly had wonderful times together.

BEE. Why shouldn't we have them again? We've proved that the date of our birth has nothing to do with our age.

BRIGADIER (*chuckling*) That's very true, my dear.

BEE. Shall we go and paint the Riviera red, Bertie?

BRIGADIER (*slowly, with delight*) You mean you'd come with me, Beatrice?

BEE. I certainly wouldn't trust you alone.

BRIGADIER. It really would be very pleasant. But, my dear, though we've reached—years of maturity, I fear tongues would wag.

BEE (*so that even he understands*) There's a way of stilling them, Bertie, dear.

BRIGADIER. Beatrice! Do you mean . . . ?

(ALICE *bursts in from the hall.*
HATTIE *and* NAN *follow her on.* NAN *closes the doors*)

ALICE (*smiling triumphantly*) I *do* hope I'm not interrupting . . .

(*The* BRIGADIER *rises and moves to the fireplace*)

BEE (*furious*) Dear Alice!

ALICE (*moving to* L *of Bee*) Lily's retired to bed with a sick headache, so we thought it an ideal time to do up some money parcels.

BRIGADIER. You're right—we're very behindhand with parcelling.

(ALICE *moves* L)

BEE. Are you sure Lily's not just pretending? (*She remains disconsolately sitting*)

HATTIE. No, she looked awful, poor thing.

NAN (*moving above the ottoman*) Anyhow, we've switched out the light in the passage, and put a bucket there.

BRIGADIER. Come along, then. I'll get my book with the addresses. (*He crosses to the plinth and takes an address book from the hiding-place*)

NAN. I'll get the money. (*She moves to the chair down* R, *picks up the cushion, then crosses and stands behind the table up* L)

ALICE. I'll get the brown paper. (*She takes some brown paper from the cabinet down* R)

(HATTIE *crosses to the desk and takes a ball of string from the drawer*)

(*She chuckles aloud at Bee and reminds her about her task*) Bee, the gloves.

(BEE *rises, takes five pairs of white cotton gloves from the barrel hiding-place on the table* R *and crosses with them to the table up* L. *They all gather round the table.* NAN *is* C, ALICE R *of Nan,* BEE R *of Alice, the* BRIGADIER L *of Nan and* HATTIE L *of the Brigadier*)

Hundred-pound parcels this time, isn't it?

HATTIE. Yes, isn't it wonderful?

ALICE. We mustn't have too long a session, they have dinner very early at my new hotel. (*She rubs her hands delightedly*) There are going to be some splendidly deserving cases there, I think.

(*They each put on a pair of white gloves*)

NAN. I wonder whether we really need these? The notes must have dozens of fingerprints.

HATTIE. They save us from germs, anyhow.

NAN. Ready? (*She empties out a mass of pound notes from the interior of the cushion*)

HATTIE. Oh, what lovely lolly! It makes me feel quite abandoned. (*She picks up a handful of notes and throws them in the air*)

BRIGADIER. Hattie, really!

(*The telephone rings*)

BEE (*kneeling to pick up the notes*) Answer it, Hattie dear.

(HATTIE *crosses to the telephone and lifts the receiver*)

(*With a handful of notes*) If it's Madame Spanager again, I can't afford a knitting machine.

HATTIE (*into the telephone*) Hullo? . . . Dame Beatrice? . . . Yes, she's here. Who is it? . . . (*When she hears, she covers the mouthpiece with her hand, gives a little scream, and stands stock still*)

BEE (*rising*) Who is it?

(HATTIE *cannot speak*)

What's the matter?

HATTIE (*gasping*) It's—it's Scotland Yard.

(*There are general gasps of horror*)

BEE (*in a whisper*) Scotland Yard! Say I'm not in. (*She backs* R)

HATTIE (*whispering*) I've just said you are.

BEE (*whispering*) Then I'm ill.

ALICE (*whispering*) No, no, you must speak.

BRIGADIER (*crossing to* L *of Bee*) It would look suspicious if you didn't.

BEE (*whispering*) But he may trap me into saying something incriminating.

NAN (*whispering*) Speak—but pretend to be deaf.

(BEE *crosses and takes the receiver from* HATTIE, *who stands behind Bee.* NAN *stands behind the table. The* BRIGADIER *is* C *with* ALICE L *of him*)

BEE (*shouting into the telephone*) This is Dame Beatrice Appleby . . . Detective-Sergeant who? . . . I'm sorry I can't catch the name . . . What? . . . I'm afraid I'm a little hard of hearing. I beg your pardon? . . . I still can't hear what you're saying . . . No, hardly a word. I'm so sorry . . . (*Suddenly dynamic*) No! No! Don't do that . . . Hullo! Inspector? Hullo. (*She replaces the receiver*) Disaster!

BRIGADIER. What? What?

BEE. He's coming round.

(*There are exclamations of alarm from the others*)

HATTIE. No! I—I feel ill—I'm going to be . . .

BEE (*hurrying to Hattie*) Don't you dare! (*She gives Hattie a little slap, then goes to each of the others in turn and collects the gloves from them*)

(*They are all panicky and move about in disorder*)

ALICE. Heavens, what are we going to do?

(ALICE *and the* BRIGADIER *help* NAN *cram the notes back into the cushion*)

BEE. Whatever it is, it must be quick.
BRIGADIER. We ought to have planned for this.
NAN (*crossly*) Well, we haven't. So think of a course of action.
HATTIE (*pointing to the ottoman*) We're sunk with all that hot fur.
BEE. We're nothing of the sort.
BRIGADIER (*dithering*) We must get rid of it somehow.
NAN (*furious*) Of course! But how?
BEE (*putting the gloves in the barrel*) Could we wrap them in paper and hide them up the bedroom chimneys?
NAN. There'd be soot clues.
ALICE. Think, everyone, think.
HATTIE (*terrified*) We're sunk. Absolutely sunk! (*In her nervousness she unravels the ball of string*)
BRIGADIER. Now, none of that defeatist talk.
ALICE (*picking up the brown paper and crossing to the cabinet down* R) What about pinned inside the curtains? (*She puts the paper in the cabinet*)

(NAN *crosses and puts the cushion on the armchair down* R)

BRIGADIER. Too bulky.
HATTIE (*crossing to* C; *getting more and more alarmed*) Behind the bath?—no. In the frig?—no. In our beds?—no. It's no good, I can't think. We shall be caught. (*Hysterically*) We shall be caught! I know it! (*She screams*) Ooh!

(NAN *crosses to Hattie and leads her to the desk chair. They both get entangled in the unravelled ball of string*)

NAN (*comforting her*) Steady, old girl, steady. (*She sits Hattie in the desk chair*)
ALICE. If only we had time to think properly . . .
BRIGADIER (*crossly*) We haven't! He may arrive at any moment.

(*The noise of a bucket crashing is heard off in the hall*)

ALICE (*in despair*) Lily! That's all we needed.

BEE (*excitedly*) Perhaps it's *just* what we need. She's had dealings with the police, she knows their ways.

(LILY *enters from the hall and closes the door behind her. She wears a dressing-gown and feathered mules*)

LILY. I heard a scream; who's done what?
BEE (*moving to Lily; lightly*) Ah, Lily! Feeling better?
LILY. No, horrible. And now I've bruised my ankle. Why the bucket?
BEE. We'll explain later.

(BEE *and the* BRIGADIER *lead* LILY *down* C)

Sit down, I have something to ask you.
LILY. Oh, not now, *please*, Dame dear.

(BEE *sits* LILY *firmly on the stool and stands* L *of her. The* BRIGADIER *stands* R *of Lily*)

BEE. Lily; you know you said you'd do anything to repay what I did when you came out of Holloway?
LILY (*suspiciously*) Yes?
BEE (*sitting in the tub chair*) Well, now I want you to stop me going into Holloway.
LILY. What! (*She looks round at the guilty circle*) Don't tell me you've been at it again?
BEE (*nodding shamefacedly*) Rather considerably "at it".
LILY. Well, knock me flat! (*She rises. Determinedly*) All right!
HATTIE. What are you going to do?
LILY. I'm giving in my notice.
HATTIE. Oh, no!
LILY (*moving towards the double doors*) And leaving before the police arrive.
BEE. You're too late; they're on their way.
LILY (*stopping and turning*) What! (*She moves to* R *of Bee. Suddenly deadly urgent*) Is that true?
BRIGADIER (*nodding*) A detective from Scotland Yard.
HATTIE. You *must* help us, Lily.
LILY (*after a moment's thought*) Have you got any stuff in the flat?
NAN. Rather a lot.
LILY (*running to the double doors*) Night, night!

(*The others all rush to Lily and detain her.* ALICE *to* R *of her,* BEE *to* L *of her, the* BRIGADIER *to* L *of Bee,* HATTIE *below the Brigadier and* NAN *to* L *of Hattie*)

HATTIE. No, you've got to save us.
LILY. I wouldn't even if my head would let me.
BEE. Please, Lily.

ALICE. I'll cure it. (*To Nan*) Water. (*She crosses and gets her handbag from the table* R)
BEE. Now, sit down.

(BEE *and the* BRIGADIER *manœuvre* LILY *into the tub chair.* NAN *gets a glass of water from the sideboard.* ALICE *crosses to* R *of Lily.* BEE *stands* L *of Lily and the* BRIGADIER *behind her.* HATTIE *moves down* L)

ALICE. One of my special migraine tablets; they're miraculous.

(ALICE *takes a bottle of pills from her bag*)

LILY. Let's see what you've got.
BRIGADIER. Key, Nan.

(HATTIE *moves up* L *and lowers the basket.* NAN *gets the key, crosses, unlocks the ottoman and opens it*)

ALICE. One of these, and you'll feel a new woman.

(ALICE *makes* LILY *swallow a pill and a sip of water*)

LILY. I'll need to.

(*The* BRIGADIER *and* NAN *show Lily the furs in the ottoman*)

(*She groans*) All that! I'd better have another. (*She swallows another tablet*)
HATTIE (*moving down* L) You will help us, won't you?
LILY (*severely*) If I did, I'd want a solemn promise from each one of you.
HATTIE. Yes, yes.
LILY. No, no, not just "yes, yes". On your sacred words. In future never to touch so much as an ermine tail.
HATTIE (*kneeling quickly*) I promise never to touch so much as an ermine tail again.
BEE. So do I.
NAN. Cross my heart.
ALICE. I promise, too.
BRIGADIER (*standing to attention*) My word—as a soldier.
HATTIE. Now, quickly, what shall we do?
LILY (*after a moment's thought*) I haven't the faintest.
BEE. Lily!
LILY. Give me time, Dame dear. The drug's only just beginning to penetrate.
BRIGADIER (*pulling himself together*) We aren't observing usual precautions. Take up position, Hattie, and watch for the police.

(HATTIE *scuttles to the window*)

Others check room for give-away clues.

(ALICE *crosses to the desk, puts down the glass, pills and handbag,* and checks the wool-basket. NAN checks the animal's head and the cushion down R. HATTIE raises the hanging-basket. The BRIGADIER checks the screen, barrel and tusk. NAN then goes generally around the room)

LILY. Well, whatever you do—(*urgently*) you must get that stuff out of the flat. If he's got a search-warrant, he'll find it.

(HATTIE *watches out of the window*)

NAN. But where could we take them?

LILY (*after a moment's thought*) Could you do one of your quick schemes, and dump them in the Spanagers' flat?

NAN (*shaking her head*) Hardly cricket.

BEE. I know. The attic where the old porter stored my antlers.

LILY (*excitedly*) Yes. Nobody ever goes up there, and I've still got the key.

BRIGADIER (*moving below the ottoman*) He'll remember if they question him.

LILY. They can't—he's in his grave.

NAN. That's it, then. Ripping!

BRIGADIER. Now, how to get them there?

HATTIE (*screaming*) Cave! The police!

BEE. What!

(*They all rush in disorder to the window*)

HATTIE. Isn't that a police car?

BEE (*moving* C) Two loudspeakers on the roof. Must be.

LILY (*crossing to* L *of Bee*) Yes, that's it. He's got a patrol car to bring him along.

BRIGADIER (*standing on the crate and peering out of the window*) That must be he; the one in the mac.

NAN. He's gone straight in.

BEE. We've got to use our wits to get out of this.

BRIGADIER (*moving down* L) It's imperative to delay him while we decide our course of action.

NAN. I'll tell you what. I'll dash downstairs, and block the lift. (*She hurries into the hall*) And send him to the wrong flat if possible.

BRIGADIER (*shouting after her*) Then hold yourself in reserve, outside the flat—in case of emergency.

(NAN *exits by the front door*)

LILY (*going to the* L *end of the ottoman*) If you can get him in this room, and keep him here, I'll nip up the fire-escape with the furs to the attic.

(*The* BRIGADIER *and* ALICE *cross to the front of the ottoman and start to take the furs out*)

E

BEE (*on* L *of Lily*) Oh, no. We daren't risk you being caught, Lily.
LILY. I'm not sure I wouldn't find Holloway a nice rest.
HATTIE. Lily, don't.

(*The* BRIGADIER *and* ALICE *put the furs into* LILY's *arms and close the ottoman*)

LILY. I'll put them in the kitchen larder while I let him in.
BEE. Good; dump them in the larder, show him in here, and leave him to us.

(LILY, *assisted through the doors by* BEE, *exits to the hall.* BEE *closes the doors. The* BRIGADIER *moves down* R. ALICE *stands below the ottoman.* HATTIE *moves down* L)

ALICE (*frantically*) But how can we keep him in here long enough for her to get up to the attic?
BEE (*moving* C; *thoughtfully*) We can be slow answering his questions—he'll expect that at our age. (*Excitedly*) Our age! That's the solution. If we behave as old people are expected to, we can detain him for hours.
ALICE. Of course! Darling, you're a genius. We'll be full of reminiscences...
BRIGADIER. Bad-tempered.
HATTIE. Vague.
BEE. Inconsequential.
BRIGADIER. Brilliant, Beatrice. Bamboozle him with age.

(*The front-door bell rings*)

HATTIE. Oh! He's here!
BRIGADIER (*rushing to* L *of the tub chair; panicking*) Don't panic! Don't panic!
HATTIE. Have I time to rush and get a spoonful of my tonic? (*She dashes towards the double doors*)
BRIGADIER (*intercepting Hattie: frantically*) No, no! (*In a loud whisper*) Now, our objective's clear? Trap him in here for at least five minutes.
BEE. Yes, yes.
BRIGADIER. No time for specific plans—act on intuition.
ALICE. We must be doing something—it's suspicious our being gathered here...
BRIGADIER. Cards! Playing bridge.
HATTIE. I don't know bridge.
BEE (*crossing to the desk*) Anyhow, I've only got patience cards. (*She takes two packs of patience cards from the desk drawer*)
ALICE. We two will be playing patience, then.

(*The front-door bell rings.*
LILY *puts her head round the double doors*)

LILY (*in a hoarse whisper*) Remember; if you don't keep him in here five minutes, you won't see me for five years.

(LILY *withdraws her head and closes the doors*)

ALICE. Quickly, Bee—the cards. Bertie, the table. (*She pulls the armchair down R to R of the ottoman and sits*)

BRIGADIER. Keep watch at the keyhole, Hattie.

HATTIE (*crossing to the double doors*) Oh, dear. (*She takes out the key and peers through the keyhole*)

(*The* BRIGADIER *moves the table down L to the ottoman.* BEE *crosses and sits at the R end of the ottoman. She and* ALICE *frantically lay out cards all over the table which is between them. The* BRIGADIER *crosses to L of Hattie*)

BEE. Has she let him in?

HATTIE (*peering through the keyhole*) The dratted fern's in the way.... She's opened the door.... Standing arms akimbo.

BRIGADIER. Good girl. I'll be engrossed in *The Times*. (*He crosses and picks up the newspaper from the desk*)

BEE. Can you see what he looks like?

HATTIE. Not for the moment. The field's very limited.

ALICE. If he's young we'll be able to embarrass him.

HATTIE. There's movement! He's in! Advancing!! (*She replaces the key and darts down C*)

BRIGADIER (*sitting in the tub chair*) Positions, everyone.

HATTIE (*moving to R of the Brigadier; in a panic*) But what is my position?

BRIGADIER (*looking around*) Let me see—let me see . . .

HATTIE (*wildly*) You've left me high and dry.

BEE (*pointing to the desk*) Be writing a letter.

HATTIE. Who to? (*She flies and sits at the desk*)

(LILY *enters from the hall and stands to one side*)

LILY. A young man to see you, Dame dear.

(DETECTIVE-SERGEANT PAPE *enters from the hall. He is a pleasant-looking young man, not very sure of himself. He is in plain clothes and a mackintosh. The four in the room age noticeably, move slowly, and speak in old voices.*

LILY *exits to the hall, closing the doors behind her.* BEE *acts very slowly, placing cards deliberately, and taking no notice of Pape*)

BEE. I think that one there. (*Triumphantly placing another card*) And that one there!

PAPE. Good afternoon. I'm Detective-Sergeant Pape of Scotland Yard.

BEE. And *that* one—there.

ALICE. And I think that one there. (*With shaking hand she tries*

E*

to see the card, and then with shaking head and hand concentrates on her game)
PAPE. I'm from Scotland Yard.
BRIGADIER *(taking no notice of Pape; very gruffly)* I see gilt-edged have fallen again.
BEE *(cupping her ear to Pape)* What did you say?
BRIGADIER *(bellowing bad-temperedly)* I said gilt-edged have fallen again.
BEE. No, no; I was asking what this young man said.
BRIGADIER *(furiously)* Never mind what *he* says. What does he know about gid-eltched? *(He shouts)* Gilt-edged. *(He tears the paper in his fury)*
BEE *(to Pape; apologetically)* You must excuse the Brigadier; his gout's very bad today. *(She points to the stool)*

(The BRIGADIER *draws the stool to him, and rests his right leg on it)*

ALICE *(reminiscing)* My dear old father used to have gout. His language! Do you know I've never dared have an anaesthetic since.
PAPE *(trying again)* I've come to see you because . . .
BEE. It's very kind of you—we don't have many visitors. *(She rises and moves to Pape, limping as if crippled with arthritis)* But come away from that door. *(She takes Pape by the arm and leads him down* C, *bumping into him at each step)* There's a terrible draught just there. Last year I had a nasty attack of bronchitis, and I put it down solely to draught.
PAPE (R *of Bee)* I fear my visit isn't social. It's connected with . . .
HATTIE *(jumping into the breach)* Tell me—how do you spell "antirrhinum"?
BEE *(limping below Pape to* R *of Hattie)* Anti what?
HATTIE. Antirrhinum. The flower.
BEE. Oh, Antirrhinum. The flower. A-N-T-E-R . . .
ALICE. No—I-R. And there's an "H" somewhere.

*(*PAPE *looks at* ALICE *who places another card, with increased shaking as she sees Pape looking at her)*

HATTIE. A-N-T-H . . . ?
BEE. No, no; the "H" comes near the end.
PAPE. If you'll forgive me interrupting . . .
BEE. Yes, of course. *(She crosses above the Brigadier to* L *of Pape)* Coming from Scotland Yard you'd know. *(She cups her ear and leans towards him)* How is it spelt?
PAPE. "Antirrhinum?"
BEE. The flower.
PAPER. Er—A-N-T-I-R—er—A-N-T-I-R-I . . .
BRIGADIER *(explosively)* No, no, no! There are two "R's". *(He*

demonstrates on his fingers) A-N-T-I-R-R—umm—A-N-T-I-R-R-umm . . .
PAPE. Why not put "snapdragon"?
HATTIE. Oh, yes. Thank you so much.
PAPE. Now, it's been reported to us that . . .
BEE (*hastily*) What did you say your name was?
PAPE. Pape.
BEE. Pape? I was at school with a Miss Pape. Daisy Pape. She had bow legs and plaits. I wonder if . . .
PAPE. Excuse me, I must get on.

(BEE *taps the Brigadier on the shoulder, crosses and stands above the ottoman*)

This report we received concerned . . .
BRIGADIER (*crashing his paper*) Bless my soul! (*He rises and stands* L *of the tub chair*)
HATTIE (*alarmed*) What is it?
BRIGADIER (*very bad-temperedly*) These damn politicians! Rushing us towards bankruptcy. Yet there's a quite simple solution. (*He looks at his watch, moves to Pape, and pulls him over to his* L) Listen to my plan; it will only take—(*with a warning glance at the others*) three minutes. It's in five phases. Phase one consists of . . .

(LILY *bursts distractedly in from the hall. All are horrified to see her*)

LILY. Dame, dear . . .
BEE (*moving to* R *of Lily; horrified*) Lily! Why aren't you getting on with—what you should be getting on with?
LILY. I *can't*, Dame dear. (*She points to Pape*) Another one's come up after him, and is standing in the hall. I can't get on with —anything.
BEE. This is too terrible!

(*The* BRIGADIER *hesitates a moment, then marches to the double doors and speaks to Kemp, off in the hall*)

BRIGADIER. Come in here, sir—I want a word with you.
PAPE (*motioning Kemp to remain*) He's all right where he is, thank you.

(*There is a pause of consternation*)

BEE (*moving above the ottoman*) I feel ill. (*The words give her an idea and she immediately goes into action*) Yes, I *do* feel ill. Terribly ill. It's one of my attacks. (*She crosses to Pape, turns her back on him, and leans back into his arms*) Help me to the sofa, quickly.
BRIGADIER (*calling into the hall*) Officer, officer, you *must* come now. Emergency.

(POLICE CONSTABLE KEMP *enters from the hall. He is a dour-looking policeman, in uniform.* ALICE *rises*)

Help lift the Dame.

(PAPE *and* KEMP *start to carry* BEE *to the ottoman,* PAPE *supporting her under her arms, and* KEMP *taking her feet*)

LILY. I'll fetch your emergency capsules from the kitchen.

(LILY *runs out by the double doors*)

HATTIE (*rising and crossing to the double doors*) Oh, poor Dame Beatrice! One of her sudden attacks. How terrible! The poor dear, the poor dear. (*During the confusion she closes the double doors*)

(*The* BRIGADIER *moves the card table above the ottoman.* ALICE *pushes the lifting party away from the ottoman each time they near it, making the animal's head the excuse*)

ALICE Slowly! Take her gently. Don't hurry—it would be very dangerous. Slower! Slower! Take plenty of time. Mind the animal. Oh, mind the animal.

(PAPE *and* KEMP *eventually lay* BEE *on the ottoman.* PAPE *stands* R *of the ottoman,* KEMP L *of it.* ALICE *and the* BRIGADIER *stand above the ottoman*)

HATTIE (*moving to the left end of the ottoman; to Bee*) Are you better, Dame Beatrice?

BEE (*weakly*) I think I shall be better in about five minutes.

(HATTIE *moves down* L)

PAPE. All right, Kemp.

(KEMP *turns to exit*)

BRIGADIER (*stopping Kemp; urgently*) Warmth—it's imperative she's kept warm. (*He pushes Kemp towards the door down* L) A rug. You'll find one in that bedroom on top of the wardrobe. I can't reach—war wound.

(*The* BRIGADIER *pushes* KEMP *off down* L)

BEE. I can't breathe. I can't breathe. Prop me up.

(PAPE *picks up the cushion from the armchair down* R. ALICE, *with a slight scream, rushes to Pape, grabs the cushion, whisks it from him, and pushes it under Bee's head.*

NAN *appears furtively on the balcony, and peers surreptitiously into the room.* HATTIE *rushes to the window, and signals Nan to stay out of sight,* NAN *disappears*)

PAPE (*firmly*) I'm sorry to be insistent, but I must . . .

ALICE (*pointing to Bee; in mock alarm at his loud voice*) Ssh! Please! The patient.

(PAPE *pauses undecidedly*)

PAPE (*in a whisper*) While she recovers I'll go and question the maid. (*He slowly and deliberately crosses below the ottoman towards the double doors*)

(*The others watch in horror, unable to think of anything else to do*)

HATTIE (*moaning*) Oh, no!

(NAN *enters the double doors as* PAPE *is about to open them, and gives a prolonged and loud scream.*

KEMP *enters down* R, *carrying a rug*)

NAN (*locking the doors*) There now I've got you. (*She puts the key in her bosom and stands spreadeagled against the doors*)

(PAPE *looks at Nan, astonished*)

BEE. Is something the matter, Nanette dear?
PAPE. Who is this lady?
BRIGADIER. Miss Parry—she lives here.
ALICE. Forgive her, she's . . . (*She taps her head*)
NAN (*looking at Kemp*) Bee, I'm so glad you sent for a policeman—(*she crosses above the ottoman*) because this is the man—(*she points to Pape*) I was telling you about.
BEE. What man, Nanette dear?
NAN (*suddenly inspired*) The man who had all those voice lessons, and went away without paying.
PAPE (*moving to* L *of Nan*) Madame, I assure you that you are mistaken . . .
NAN (*interrupting*) It's no use denying it. I'd recognize your bad consonants anywhere.
PAPE. Recognize my what?
NAN (*appalled*) "Recognize my what" not "Recernize me wot." All those lessons, and you're as bad as ever. There's a "G" in recognize. Let's hear it—"Recognize". Come along. Repeat.
PAPE. Now, look here . . .
NAN (*clapping her hands*) No. No, repeat. Take a deep breath— (*she puts her hand on Pape's diaphragm*) and let me hear "recognize" ten times.

(*There is a knock on the door.* KEMP *hands the rug to the Brigadier*)

BEE. Lily! We must let her in, Nanette dear.
NAN. But what about this welsher?
BEE. He's not Welsh, he's Scotland Yard.
NAN. Oh. (*She takes out the key, gives it to Pape, then crosses to the fireplace*)

(PAPE *gives the key to* KEMP *who unlocks and opens the door.*

LILY *rushes in from the hall, carrying a glass of water, and goes to Bee.* PAPE *nods to Kemp.*

KEMP *exits to the hall. The* BRIGADIER *crosses to* L *of the otto-*

man with the rug. ALICE *stands above the ottoman.* HATTIE *moves down* L)

LILY. Couldn't find the capsules anywhere. So I've brought soda-bicarbonate instead. Now, don't worry—(*meaningly*) everything's all right.

BEE (*waving the glass aside*) Thank you. But I suddenly feel better. (*She sits up*)

PAPE (*grimly*) Then perhaps, at last, we can get down to business.

BEE. Business, Inspector?

(*They all drop their "age-act" from now on.* HATTIE *sits in the tub chair. The* BRIGADIER *puts the rug on the ottoman.* LILY *puts the glass on the sideboard*)

PAPE (*taking out his notebook*) Now, as you are all probably aware, there have lately been several serious fur robberies. They're carried out by an extremely well-organized gang.

HATTIE (*trembling*) Gang!

PAPE. A gang which we're determined to find and break up.

BRIGADIER. Oh?

PAPE. We're on their track, and follow up every clue.

ALICE. Oh.

PAPE. So when we were given this address in connection with fur robberies . . .

HATTIE. Oh! (*She lets out a scream before she can cover her mouth with her hand*)

PAPE (*moving to* R *of Hattie*) Are you the lady concerned?

HATTIE (*terrified*) Yes, I am! I mean, no, I'm not! At least . . .

PAPE. Well, are you or not?

HATTIE (*out of control*) Yes, I am, but—oh, dear—I—I—this is terrible, ghastly. (*To the others. In complete panic*) He obviously knows everything. We'd better confess.

PAPE (*alert*) Confess? Confess what?

BRIGADIER (*urgently*) Take no notice of her.

NAN. The poor beast's a bit under the weather.

PAPE (*moving close to Hattie*) What did you mean? What is there to confess?

HATTIE (*terrified*) Nothing!

PAPE (*pressing*) But you admitted there was. Come along, tell me what it is.

HATTIE (*rising*) No! There isn't anything. At least . . . (*She screams hysterically and looks to the desk*) Oh, I can't bear this cat-and-mouse any longer.

BRIGADIER. Hattie!

HATTIE (*loudly to Pape*) We are responsible. We'll tell the whole truth . . .

BEE (*rising; with immense authority*) Hattie—stop it! (*Quietly*) I will not have hysterics. Lily, my smelling-salts in my bag. (*She points to the desk*)

(LILY *crosses to the desk, takes the smelling-salts from Bee's bag, and thrusts them under Hattie's nose*)

PAPE (*sternly*) But I *want* the whole truth, my lady.
BEE. You shall have it.
NAN. Steady.
BRIGADIER. Beatrice, I think . . .
BEE (*moving to* R *of Pape; in complete command*) I will do the explaining.

(*There is a short pause*)

PAPE. Yes, my lady?
BEE. As you've gathered, we *have* something to confess.
ALICE. Darling, for goodness' sake . . .
BEE (*to Pape*) But I am the *only* one who might be charged.
BRIGADIER. No, Beatrice, I won't allow it.
NAN } (*together*) { Neither will I . . .
HATTIE } { (*Weakly*) Me, me . . .

(ALICE *and* LILY *move forward*)

ALICE } (*together*) { It's dear of you, but . . .
LILY } { All right, all right, leave it to me.
BEE (*imperiously*) Quiet, all of you! (*To Pape*) As I was saying —I am solely responsible. So if you are ready, I will accompany you to Scotland Yard. (*She moves up to the double doors*)

(*The others watch in horror*)

PAPE. Before we do that, my lady, I think . . . (*He sees Nan's mole coat on he chair* L *of the doors and breaks off*) Wait a moment! What's this? (*He picks up the coat and examines it*) This looks remarkably like the coat stolen from the *Pink Parakeet* tearoom this morning.
HATTIE. Oh!
LILY (*in a whisper to Hattie*) Ssh, or I'll slap you.
PAPE (*consulting his notebook*) "Mole, lined coffee crêpe, with darker embroidered branch design." (*He looks round at the others*) That's odd. This is the coat I came to enquire about.

(*The others stare in amazement at Pape*)

BEE (*moving to Pape; slowly*) The coat you came to enquire about?
PAPE. Yes. The manager of the tearoom reported that the lady created such a scene that he never got her name. Only that she lived with a Dame Beatrice Appleby at this address. I rang up to find out, but as you couldn't hear me, I came round to check particulars.
BEE (*aghast*) And that's the only thing you've come about?

PAPE. The only thing I *came* about, my lady. (*Severely*) But your confession, and finding the stolen coat here, alters the situation.
BEE (*after a moment's thought*) But that's easy to explain. And what I was going to Scotland Yard *to* explain. You see, it's Miss Parry's. Miss Hatfield and I went to the tearoom and saw the coat lying abandoned there. Knowing our friend to be very absent-minded, we thought she'd left it by mistake. So we picked it up and brought it home.
PAPE (*doubtfully*) Oh? (*He crosses below the ottoman to Nan*) Are you the lady? And is this your coat?
NAN. Yes. You'll find a hanky with my initials in the pocket.

(PAPE *takes a handkerchief from the coat pocket*)

PAPE. "N.A.P."
NAN. Nanette Angelica Parry.
PAPE (*crossing to* C; *puzzled*) But why was—(*he points to Hattie*) this lady so scared, and why have you all behaved so oddly?
BEE. Well—(*she thinks frantically*) we were terrified you'd think we were part of this well-organized gang you told us about.
PAPE. There was never much fear of that.
NAN. I should jolly well hope not.
BEE. So all is happily settled then, Inspector Pape?
PAPE (*putting the coat on the chair*) I shall have to explain to my chief, but I think he'll understand.
BRIGADIER. I'm sure he will. Give the fellow a cup of tea, Beatrice.
BEE. Lily, give them both a cup of tea. Give them everything you've got *left* in the larder.
PAPE (*moving and opening the double doors*) That's very kind, my lady. Just a very quick cup. I'll try not to trouble you again. Good afternoon.
ALL (*ad lib.*) Good afternoon.

(PAPE *exits to the hall*)

LILY (*in a whisper*) A fine reward for faithful service—tea with two cops!

(LILY *exits to the hall, closing the doors behind her*)

NAN. Christmas!
BEE (*moving* C) Heavens be praised!

(NAN *crosses to* R *of Bee*)

ALICE. Oh, the relief!
BRIGADIER (*crossing to* RC) By Jove, that was a near one.
HATTIE (*sitting in the desk chair*) I'm so ashamed I could cry.
NAN. Cry! I could dance. (*She dances a few steps down* L) Tollderolloll.

ACT III BREATH OF SPRING 71

BRIGADIER (*to Bee*) You were magnificent, my dear, absolutely magnificent.

(*All join in the praises*)

(*Fondly*) You've certainly earned that holiday on the Riviera we talked about. (*Meaningly*) When I draw up the rosters, I shall see that I have the honour of escorting you.

BEE. You mean . . . ? (*She embraces the Brigadier*) Thank you, Bertie, my dear. (*Over his shoulder*) Sorry, Alice!

ALICE (*moving to R of the Brigadier*) There's many a slip. I shall fight. And no holds barred.

NAN. When my holiday comes, I shall go to the Costa Brava.

HATTIE. Somewhere very, very quiet for me.

ALICE (*crossing above the ottoman to R*) I shall fly to Paris. I've often thought we might open a branch there. (*Her gaiety suddenly vanishes*) Oh! But we've promised to stop.

(*They are all suddenly downcast*)

NAN. Of course. How terrible! Think—we shan't be able to send any more money parcels.

HATTIE. Oh, how awful.

BEE. And the list of deserving cases as long as ever.

BRIGADIER. It's most distressing.

NAN. Takes all the gilt off the gingerbread.

BEE. It's tragic.

(*They stand mournfully for a few seconds*)

(*Suddenly*) Of course, we only promised not to have anything more to do with *furs*.

ALICE. Of course! There must be other ways of collecting funds.

BEE (*gaily*) And I think I know one.

BRIGADIER (*right back on military form*) Gather round for briefing.

(BEE *sits in the tub chair. The others gather round her as the* CURTAIN *starts to fall*)

BEE. Well, my idea is this. We . . .

The CURTAIN *falls*

FURNITURE AND PROPERTY LIST

ACT I

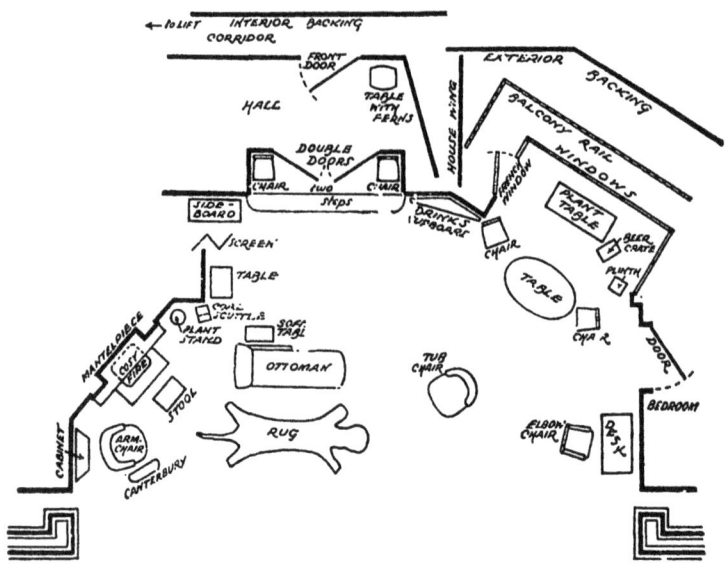

On stage: Desk. *On it:* telephone, inkwell, blotter, writing-paper, pen, pencil, ashtray, a copy of *The Times*, notebook, table-lamp
Elbow chair
On wall over desk: picture on hinge concealing Map A
Tub chair (LC)
Oval table (up LC) *On it:* cloth, bowl of flowers
4 upright chairs
Plinth with secret opening
Beer crate
Plant-table. *On it:* plants
On floor above plant-table: watering-can
Hanging from ceiling of window alcove: 2 plants, one on a pulley
Drinks cupboard. *On it:* ornament, 2 small jugs
    In it: 2 brandy glasses 5 champagne glasses
Sideboard. *In it:* tablecloth, table mats, cutlery, condiments
Folding screen
Small table. *On it:* table-lamp, ashtray
On wall above table R: small barrel. *In it:* 5 pairs of white gloves, each pair loosely joined with cotton

> *On wall above fireplace:* elephant's tusk with secret opening for hiding papers
> *On mantelpiece:* mirror, clock, invitation cards, box with cigarettes, lighter, ashtray
> "Cosy stove"
> Tool for working raker of stove
> *On wall below fireplace:* parasol with false handle for hiding key to ottoman
> Fire-stool with hidden pocket under seat
> Plant stand. *On it:* plant
> Coal scuttle
> Cabinet (down R) *On it:* ornament for hiding bell in
> Armchair (down R) *On it:* cushion with pound notes in it. (Poppers one side for easy opening)
> Newspaper rack. *In it:* papers and magazines
> Ottoman, to open up stage, with lock and key
>> *On it:* cushion
>> *Hanging in front:* work-bag with embroidery and Bee's spectacles
> Rug with head to open easily for hiding notebooks
> Table (behind ottoman) *On it:* ashtray, box with cigarettes, lighter, textbook
> Bell push above fireplace
> Window curtains
> Carpet on floor
> *In hall:* table with bowl of ferns

Windows closed
Front door closed
Door down L closed
Double doors open
Curtains open
Table-lamps on
Stove on

Off stage: Clip-board with papers (BRIGADIER)
Bottle of brandy (LILY)
Tray. *On it:* bottle of Veuve Cliquot, napkin (LILY)
Fur cape (LILY)
Rockingham teapot covered with strips of brown paper (HATTIE)
Patent pinger (BRIGADIER)
Crumpled sheet of *Radio Times* (HATTIE)
Bowl of salad (LILY)
Whistle on cord (HATTIE)

Personal: BRIGADIER: hat, gloves, umbrella, watch, butcher's apron, handkerchief
ALICE: handbag. *In it:* compact

ACT II

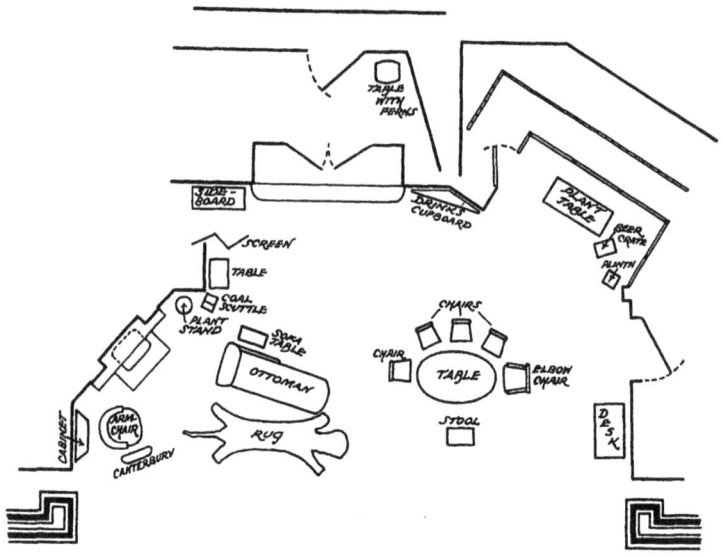

Strike: Tub-chair, "order" cards, everything from table up L, brandy bottle, champagne bottle, glasses, tray, napkin, sheet from *Radio Times*

Reset: Table up L to down LC. *On it:* 5 notebooks with pencils attached, 4 reports, clip-board with "orders", brass handbell, water carafe and glass, ashtray
Fire-stool below table LC, with open end of pocket down stage
Upright chair R of table
3 upright chairs above table
Desk chair L of table
Open out screen, the folding flap hiding Map "B"
Angle ottoman to fireplace

Set: On plant table: 4 hydrangea plants
On floor R of table: Alice's handbag
On floor below desk: wool-basket with knitting needles
In desk drawer: chessboard
In jug on cabinet up LC: 4 chessmen
On sideboard: book
On table behind ottoman: bowl of autumn flowers
In parasol handle: key to ottoman
Windows open
Front door closed

Door down L closed
Double doors closed
Curtains open
Table-lamps off
Stove on

Off stage: Elaborate hat, veil, hairpins, gloves, handbag (BEE)
Pinger, map case, whistle, binoculars (BRIGADIER)
Haversack. *In it:* 2 flag markers, ring in box (BRIGADIER)
Shopping net. *In it:* eggs, oranges (NAN)
Ermine coat (BEE)

Personal: BRIGADIER: watch
NAN: watch, handkerchief
ALICE: watch, handbag
HATTIE: watch
BEE: watch, handbag. *In it:* car key, list of timings, handkerchief, coins, receipt, smelling-salts

ACT III

Strike: Newspapers, chessboard, chessmen, flowers, hydrangeas, water carafe and glass, book. *From plinth:* haversack, map case, binoculars, pinger, whistle
From ottoman: shopping net, ermine coat
From stove: hat
Everything from table above ottoman

Reset: Table above ottoman to down L. *On it:* pencil, tickets, clipboard, list of furs, pinger, pins
Desk chair above table down L
Upright chair below cabinet up LC
Upright chair above door down L
Fold screen

Set: Tub chair LC. *On it:* furs with tickets
On stool R *of tub chair:* furs with tickets
In ottoman: Canadian ranch mink, jasmine mink, chinchilla stole, mink shrug cape. Key in lock, lid open
In cabinet down R: brown paper
On table R: Alice's handbag. *In it:* bottle of pills
On sideboard: glass of water
In plinth: address book
On desk: 2 pens, bottle of ink, copy of *The Times*, Bee's handbag with smelling-salts
In drawer: 2 packs of patience cards, ball of string
Spring flowers

Windows closed
Front door closed
Door down L closed
Double doors closed
Curtains open
Table-lamps off
Stove off

Off stage: Mole coat, plastic raincoat (HATTIE)
Rug (KEMP)
Glass of water (LILY)

Personal: BEE: scissors on ribbon, tape-measure
BRIGADIER: watch
PAPE: notebook

The furs for the London production came from M. PRAGER LTD, 16 St Cuthbert's Road, N.W.2. Tel.: 01 452 9974 (*Breath of Spring* mink and chinchilla).

In the event of the furs described in Act III not being obtainable, other furs as luxurious as possible, can be substituted. In this case the dialogue at the beginning of Act III *describing them must* be altered to suit.

LIGHTING PLOT

Property fittings required: 2 table-lamps, stove
    Interior. A living-room. The same scene throughout
    THE APPARENT SOURCES OF LIGHT are, in daytime, windows up
    and at night, table-lamps R and L
    THE MAIN ACTING AREAS cover the whole stage

ACT I.   A spring evening
To open: Lamps on
           Evening effect outside windows
           Stove on
No cues

ACT II.   Afternoon
To open: Lamps off
           Effect of bright sunshine
           Stove lit
No cues

ACT III.   Afternoon
To open: Lamps off
           Effect of bright sunshine
No cues

EFFECTS PLOT

ACT I

Cue 1	NAN: "... I'm mad." Front-door bell rings	(Page 3)
Cue 2	LILY: "... I don't mind." Front-door bell rings	(Page 3)
Cue 3	LILY: "... than you are." Front-door bell rings	(Page 3)
Cue 4	ALICE enters Sound of party noises	(Page 3)
Cue 5	BRIGADIER: "... and it hasn't gone off yet." A loud ping	(Page 11)
Cue 6	ALICE: "Or alarmingly suspicious." Telephone rings	(Page 21)
Cue 7	BEE: "Bertie?" Stop telephone	(Page 21)
Cue 8	HATTIE: "I hope it wasn't something important." The pinger pings loudly	(Page 21)
Cue 9	HATTIE: "... a young lamb." 2 rings on front-door bell	(Page 24)

ACT II

Cue 10	LILY exits Front door slams	(Page 35)
Cue 11	BRIGADIER: "... By jove, I've a good mind to ..." The pinger goes off with a loud ping	(Page 41)
Cue 12	NAN: "... some breathing exercises." Three loud knocks on front door	(Page 45)
Cue 13	ALICE: "... out of expenses." Front-door bell rings	(Page 46)
Cue 14	LILY: "... thought down with." Front-door bell rings once. Then again	(Page 49)

ACT III

Cue 15	BRIGADIER: "Hattie, really!" Telephone rings	(Page 57)
Cue 16	BRIGADIER: "... at any moment." Noise of bucket crashing	(Page 58)
Cue 17	BRIGADIER: "... him with age." Front-door bell rings	(Page 62)
Cue 18	ALICE: "... playing patience, then." Front-door bell rings	(Page 62)

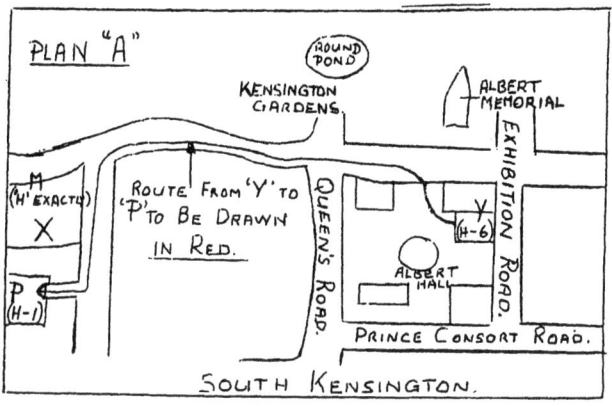

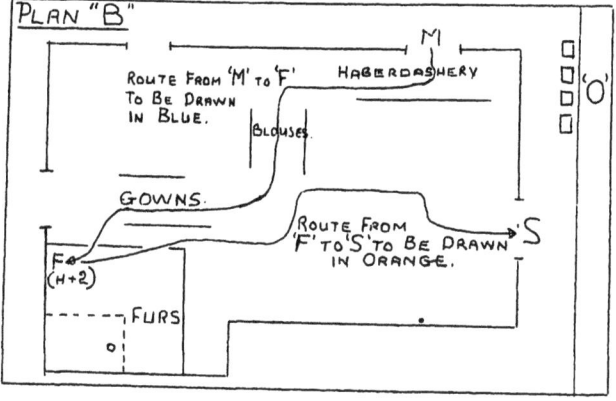

www.ingramcontent.com/pod-product-compliance
Ingram Content Group UK Ltd.
Pitfield, Milton Keynes, MK11 3LW, UK
UKHW021845210426
5322IPUK00022B/473